Crash Course in Strategic Planning

Recent Titles in
Libraries Unlimited Crash Course Series

Crash Course in Library Gift Programs: The Reluctant Curator's Guide to Caring for Archives, Books, and Artifacts in a Library Setting
Ann Roberts

Crash Course in Teen Services
Donna P. Miller

Crash Course in Reference
Charlotte Ford

Crash Course in Serving Spanish Speakers
Salvador Avila

Crash Course in Storytime Fundamentals
Penny Peck

Crash Course in Cataloging for Non-Catalogers: A Casual Conversation on Organizing Information
Allison G. Kaplan

Crash Course in Library Services to People with Disabilities
Ann Roberts and Richard Smith

Crash Course in Library Services to Preschool Children
Betsy Diamant-Cohen

Crash Course in Public Administration
Wayne Disher

Crash Course in Genealogy
David R. Dowell

Crash Course in Family Literacy Programs
Rosemary Chance and Laura Sheneman

Crash Course in Services for Seniors
Ann Roberts and Stephanie G. Bauman

Crash Course in Strategic Planning

Stephen A. Matthews and
Kimberly D. Matthews

Crash Course

LIBRARIES UNLIMITED
AN IMPRINT OF ABC-CLIO, LLC
Santa Barbara, California • Denver, Colorado • Oxford, England

Library of Congress Cataloging-in-Publication Data

Matthews, Stephen A.
Crash course in strategic planning / Stephen A. Matthews and Kimberly D. Matthews.
pages cm. — (Crash course)
Includes bibliographical references and index.
ISBN 978-1-59884-482-5 (pbk.) — ISBN 978-1-61069-059-1 (ebook)
1. Library planning. 2. Strategic planning. I. Matthews, Kimberly D. II. Title.
Z678.M385 2013
025.1—dc23 2013009850

ISBN: 978-1-59884-482-5
EISBN: 978-1-61069-059-1

17 16 15 14 13 1 2 3 4 5

This book is also available on the World Wide Web as an eBook.
Visit www.abc-clio.com for details.

Libraries Unlimited
An Imprint of ABC-CLIO, LLC

ABC-CLIO, LLC
130 Cremona Drive, P.O. Box 1911
Santa Barbara, California 93116-1911

This book is printed on acid-free paper ∞

Manufactured in the United States of America

To Peggy, wife and mother, with whose support, encouragement and participation everything has been possible, especially this book. We love you.

To Blanche Woolls, Libraries Unlimited Editor, whose expert advice and consistent shepherding enabled us to navigate this none too simple world of publishing. We appreciate you.

To All Librarians everywhere working hard to transform their libraries into a 21st Century Library. We salute you and hope this book will help.

CONTENTS

Introduction xi

Chapter 1—Why Develop a Strategic Plan 1
Theory 1
Strategic Plan Importance 2
Frequent Drastic Changes 2
Your Strategic Plan 3
Practice 3
Derailment 4
Small Library Ideas 4

Chapter 2—The 21st Century Library Strategic Plan Model 7
Theory 7
The Strategic Plan Process 7
Practice 9
Process of Inclusion 10
Additional Benefits 10
Derailment 11
Small Library Ideas 11

Chapter 3—Mission Statement 13
Theory 13
Mission 13
Mission Statement Template 13
The Statement 16
Practice 16
Determining Where You Are Now 16
Building Consensus 17
Organizational Influences 17
21st Century Library Example 18
Mission Statement 18
Assessment 18
Derailment 18
Small Library Ideas 19

Chapter 4—Values and Guiding Principles 21
Theory 21
Values and Guiding Principles Descriptors 22
Practice 22
Examples 24
A Sample Statement 25
Assessment 25
Derailment 25
Small Library Ideas 26

Chapter 5—Vision Statement 27
Theory 27
Vision 28
Vision Statement Template 29
Vision Descriptors 29
Practice 30
The Question 31

Example 31
Sample Vision Statement 31
Assessment 31
Derailment 31
Small Library Ideas 32

Chapter 6—Forecast 33
Theory 33
Forecasting the Perfect Storm 33
Forecasting Using Environmental Scan 35
STEP Analysis 35
SWOT Analysis 37
Incorporating SWOT Results 38
Incorporating the Environmental Scan Results 38
Practice 39
Derailment 39
Small Library Ideas 40

Chapter 7—Goals and Objectives 41
Theory 41
What's the Difference? 41
Goal versus Objective 42
Developing Goals 42
Practice 43
More Theory 44
Developing Objectives 44
More Practice 46
Still More Theory 47
Incorporating Opportunity 47
Planned Abandonment 47
Still More Practice 48
Sample Goals and Objectives for Strategic Partnerships 48
Derailment 49
Small Library Ideas 50

Chapter 8—Activities 51
Theory 51
Practice 53
Examples 54
Derailment 55
Small Library Ideas 56

Chapter 9—Measures and Outcomes 57
Theory 58
Measures and Outcomes 58
Measures 60
Outcomes 60
Targets and Indicators 61
Practice 61
Example 62
Derailment 64
Small Library Ideas 65

Chapter 10—Resource Allocation 67
Theory 67
Calculations 68

Priorities 69
Resources 69
Practice 69
Prioritization 69
Personnel Costs 70
Financial Costs 70
Associated Costs 71
Derailment. 71
Small Library Ideas. 72

Chapter 11—Organization of a Plan Document 73
Theory 73
Practice 74
Outside Considerations 75
Example 75
Derailment. 78
Small Library Ideas. 78

Chapter 12—Choose Your Strategic Plan Ending 79
"Choose Your Strategic Plan Ending". 80
Path C 82
Path D 83
Path E 84
Path F 85
Path G 86
Path H 86
Path J 87
Path M 88
Path O 88
Path P 89
Path R 89
Path T 90
Path U 91
Path Z 92

Chapter 13—Conclusion 93
Change Within Your Library 93
The Planning Process 94
Execution of Your Plan 95
Becoming a 21st Century Library 96

Bibliography 97

Index 99

INTRODUCTION

A HIGHLY SUCCESSFUL STRATEGIC PLAN

Right this minute, honestly answer these questions to yourself.

- Is my library implementing a strategy that is a coherent and deliberate path to fulfilling our **mission**?
- Are we utilizing our limited resources as effectively as we could be?
- Are my library's resources correctly allocated to specific **activities** that accomplish **objectives** that support **goals** that will achieve our mission?
- Is my library's mission really as visionary as it could be?
- Is my library's **vision** what we really want to become in the future?
- Next year, do I want my library to be more than it is today?
- Are we as relevant to our community as we could or should be?

If you are unable to answer "yes" to all these basic questions, then your library is not achieving its full potential, and is wasting resources just as surely as it is failing to accomplish its mission as successfully as you would like.

You must be searching for some insight into how you can take your library from where it is now to become something more. You must be interested in helping your library create a **strategic plan** that will move you forward to become a 21st Century Library. That is a commendable goal, and one that deserves the detailed ideas and recommendations that are in this book. There is no easy path to that ambition, but the simplest advice is to develop a strategy and a plan.

This book presents a coherent and logical process to tackle this monumental task of creating a highly successful strategic plan for becoming the future library you envision. A highly successful strategic plan provides all of the elements necessary to make it happen, not just allow it to happen, but to make it happen. Without a useful strategic plan any organization will flounder because it has no rudder to guide its activities toward goals, no structure to allocate critically limited resources to complete activities that achieve objectives and goals that ultimately achieve the mission. Allocating resources here and there as current pressures sway decisions does not accomplish any specific goal, and not accomplishing specific goals will not lead to accomplishing your library's mission. Think about it.

Your library's current strategic plan may be just a paper document that sits on a shelf. You are obviously interested in a highly successful plan to guide your activities and resource allocations that will achieve goals, and ultimately your library's mission. Having a strategic plan that points the way toward your vision of what you want your library to become seems like a no-brainer.

You are probably asking yourself: "What should my library look like in this 21st Century environment? What are the goals, objectives, and activities we should be accomplishing in a 21st Century Library?" Those are questions for you, your library team, and stakeholders to answer for your library. Every library's vision is specific to it. An organization's staff and planning group have many approaches to developing a strategic plan, but the one described in this book is one that implements the strongest process and provides the greatest potential for success.

THE THEORY AND PRACTICE OF A STRATEGIC PLAN

Just like in business, government, education, manufacturing, and all other professions that depend on planning, a library cannot be highly successful without one. In preparing a strategic plan for your library, it is important to understand both the theory and the practice of this most valuable tool. This book discusses and provides helpful information that will create a guide for strategic planning in the 21st Century environment.

J.R. Kidd was a Canadian educator who came to prominence in the 1960s with his ideas about adult education. Among the many ideas he wrote, one stands out as a guiding principle in virtually all endeavors. Theory without practice is empty, and practice without theory is blind (Kidd, 1973). In order to be successful, one must understand the theory of their profession as well as the practice of it. The same principle holds true with creating and implementing a highly successful strategic plan.

The elements of a strategic planning process are based on a fundamental **theory**. Why is a Mission Statement important? What value does a Vision Statement bring to an organization? What's the difference between goals and objectives? How do measures and outcomes benefit your mission accomplishment?

An equally important **practice** side of the strategic planning process helps ensure success. How do I deal with disinterested employees who don't want to contribute to developing the strategic plan? I'm already too busy, why do I have to go through all of these steps? Can't I just skip to jotting down some goals and disseminate them to my staff? Can we really guide our library from a plan on paper?

This book presents both perspectives of strategic planning: theory and practice. Most strategic planning processes fail because they are based entirely on theory and overlook the real-world practice that will lead to creating a highly successful plan. Creating a strategic plan that will be highly successful when implemented is the greatest tool any library organization can possess. A strategic plan that can be implemented in a highly successful manner can be a make-or-break tool for your library to succeed in the uncertain future that is the 21st Century.

If your approach to developing a strategic plan has always been, "Every library is supposed to have one," your experience has probably been a frustrating and futile exercise that results in a strategic plan that then sits on the shelf. Developing a highly successful strategic plan relies on having a plan that your library will actually implement to achieve goals that result in accomplishing your mission. Just as leadership is more of an art than a science, so too is developing a strategic plan to guide you to achieving your library's vision and accomplishing your mission.

CREATING YOUR HIGHLY SUCCESSFUL STRATEGIC PLAN

Strategic plans have as many styles and forms as there are libraries. Creating one that works for you is important because your plan must be something that you will actually use, and that will benefit your library from the significant amount of work that went into developing it. Some believe that a strategic plan is distinct from a master plan that simply looks at the current situation and envisions future needs, or that a strategic plan uses the end vision of what you want to become and works backward to chart a means to make that happen. Others believe that a strategic planning process can be a fun exercise in creativity in several stages of convergent thinking (Sukovic, 2011). Still others use an interpretive planning process that attempts to adopt a user perspective to develop goals and objectives that focus on the benefits of the organization to their users (Parman, 2004). Still others believe effective strategic planning can be accomplished very quickly, easily, and painlessly (Johnson & Smith, 2006). The latter seems difficult to seriously invest in.

While there may be some merit in other approaches to developing a strategic plan, deciding why your library exists, what your library values, and what your library wants to become is the most significant foundation to developing a highly successful strategic plan. Being able to actually implement your plan and use it to guide your organization to accomplish its mission is critical to making your planning highly successful. This book provides a structured approach in theory and practice, useable by any library organization to establish the basic framework for you to develop a strategic plan for your library to become everything your community needs from a 21st Century Library.

TIME SPAN FOR YOUR STRATEGIC PLAN

In the past, most librarians have invested in a strategic plan that covered five years. *Whew! We only have to do this exercise once every five years.* However, given the nature of change, as well as the pace of change within librarianship, it seems more reasonable to prepare a strategic plan every three years, or even two years. You will see as you embark on the forecast portion of this planning process that forecasting the future is vague at best, and very difficult at worst.

No hard and fast rule exists for how many years your strategic plan should cover unless your city, county, board of trustees, or other regulatory agencies have guidelines. Whatever time span for a strategic plan is prescribed will be the one you use. If it is as long as five years, you may find planning becomes more guesswork than informed or educated estimation of the future environment.

As you look outside your organization at changes in technology, society, and other external factors, you will find that these influences are in a constant state of change and predicting where that change will be in two years is virtually impossible, let alone in five years. The forecast is the most influential part of the process, therefore the most necessary. Nailing down some specific details upon which to base your predictions will be vital to providing information upon which you can base goals and objectives. Using a horizon that is as visible, yet as distant as possible, will provide a plan that is both useful and stable for the majority of the plan's time span.

TIME FOR YOUR STRATEGIC PLAN PROCESS

The next question is undoubtedly, "How long will this whole process take my staff and the others involved in the process?" Of course, the answer is "That depends." It depends on how many people will be involved, how much training will be needed to prepare for each phase of the process, how extensive your forecast will be based on your resources, and how much change you expect to accomplish. The last issue is probably the most significant factor in how long it will take your staff to develop a new strategic plan.

If the change is minimal, if your staff is relatively comfortable with planning processes, if you keep tabs regularly on external environment factors, if you are developing a two-year plan, or if you intend to do everything internally, odds are you can complete the process to a new strategic plan in less than six months. As each phase becomes more involved, as staff require more time to adjust to the changes, as outside agencies become involved to provide input or information, or if you are developing a totally new five-year plan, it might take a year to complete.

The degree of change is probably the most critical factor to how long it will take your staff to proceed. The less change, the less time it will take. The more change, the longer it will take. That is an issue that you or other leaders will have to decide on a case-by-case basis. In a large library organization with several departments, change may occur at a different pace in different departments. In smaller libraries, this will involve much smaller numbers. This can only be judged as you begin the process and devote your energies and resources to making it happen for your library.

The important thing is that you keep the process progressing, not just moving along but truly progressing. As a wise person once said; "It takes as long as it takes." Ideally, most participants will be able to complete this strategic planning process in about six months. If you can sustain progress during a longer process, then that's how long it will take.

STRATEGIC PLANNING WITHOUT ORGANIZATIONAL CHANGE

Strategic planning without organizational change would be an enigma or a paradox, whichever term you choose. Using the 21st Century Library Strategic Plan Model and process discussed in this book, it would not be easy to develop a strategic plan without going through any noticeable organizational change, although, historically, hundreds, maybe even thousands, of librarians do strategic planning without change routinely and repeatedly.

Organizational change is not the horror mystery that many authors make it out to be, but realistically, it's not the easiest thing to do in any organization. It's mostly about leadership, common sense, and knowing your people, while having a clear vision of your future in sight.

If you read any professional literature regarding organizational change, you'll read about change agents, people who make the change happen (Miller, 2002). You'll also read about culture change, and what makes an organization's culture change or resist change (Kotter, 1995). Beyond all the academics and research about change, the most important thing about successful change is that an organization wants to change, and its leadership is capable of leading it to become the more effective organization that provides better service, and is more relevant to its community.

Most directors avoid any conversation about change, and prefer to hope that it happens naturally. Unfortunately, natural change is so slow to occur as to be almost imperceptible, and is often achieved through attrition. Long serving staff members who often have helped shape the organization's culture and processes leave and allow others to fulfill that role and introduce changes. Libraries in the 21st Century do not have the luxury to allow change naturally, not if they want to remain relevant to their community that is changing dramatically due to social and technology forces with their own rapidly advancing timetable.

The 21st Century Library Strategic Plan Model will enable you and your library staff to accomplish change in a consensus-building environment, to create your innovative mission, to ensure participation from key individuals, and to include new ideas for goals and objectives. It will enable you to develop a truly living document to guide your library toward its 21st Century Library vision.

CHAPTER 1

Why Develop a Strategic Plan

THEORY

Technology is changing. Customers are changing. Employees are changing. Communities are changing. Doing things the way we've always done them is shortsighted and impractical in the face of drastic 21st Century change. Strategies and processes that worked in the past will not be as effective in the future because both the internal and external environments are dramatically changing. At best, old methods will lead to stagnation, which will leave your library further behind what it should be to survive in the current environment. At worst, maintaining a status quo will lead to your library becoming irrelevant to your community, and eventually to its closure.

A strategic plan requires you to consider the changes in your environment, and to establish and prioritize goals and objectives, which will achieve your mission and vision in the face of these challenges. Remember that a strategic plan:

- is proactive to prevent being reactive;
- communicates a common vision for the library stakeholders;
- creates the right balance between what the organization is capable of versus what the organization desires to do;
- addresses major issues (i.e., internal and external factors) at a macro level;
- manages change within the library;
- prevents excessive inward-focused and short-term thinking;
- establishes priorities that accomplish the library's mission;
- helps to better focus activities and resources on the mission; and
- guides decision making at all levels—strategic, action, and individual.

Strategic Plan Importance

The first principle of strategic planning is that it is about change. Organizational change promoted by individual change. That is also the first derailment point. If the people and organization cannot change, this strategic plan will not help you. If your previous experience with a strategic plan is that it is no big deal and a relatively easy process, you may be asking yourself, "How in the world can a strategic plan possibly be that valuable?" and/or "How can it be worth all that time and effort?" The answer is simple. It is THE BEST method to ensure that you accomplish the goals you have established to achieve the mission you have determined is essential. You must recognize that everything contained in this strategic plan is designed and oriented toward achieving the library's mission—EVERYTHING! Nothing is superfluous!

If there is an activity that does not contribute to an objective to achieve a goal, then it should not be in the plan! If your plan has traditional activities that some staff person has always done and been allowed to do because they appear somewhat productive even though outdated, you are allowing valuable resources to be expended to accomplish activities that contribute to WHAT objective to accomplish WHAT goal? If you have activities that you perform every day or month or year that are not encompassed in objectives and goals, your organization probably skipped over some essential steps in the plan development that everyone thought were a waste of time. In either case—you are wasting resources, and you've miscalculated your objectives and goals and are jeopardizing your mission accomplishment (Feinman, 1999).

General George S. Patton is credited with saying that a bad plan violently executed now is better than the perfect plan too late. While that sounds bold, decisive, and expedient, forget it. That approach does not apply to your library strategic plan. If you have a bad plan that you are trying to enthusiastically execute, it won't work. In Patton's situation, a battle plan is only good until the first shot is fired when it all then becomes about strength of forces, troop maneuver, and communications. In your library, a bad plan can only make the situation worse if any one of your staff is trying to execute a plan that is not understood, in which no one is invested, and doing tasks that consume limited resources but do not contribute to an objective or goal, and ultimately the mission. Other staff members are probably just ignoring the plan because they know it is useless. Anything you don't use is useless.

Why does this approach to developing a strategic plan go into such detail? Quite simply because that is the only way to ensure that what the library staff DOES—each individual activity—contributes to the mission. The only way to ensure that limited library resources are being appropriately applied to accomplish that mission is to ensure that they are applied to the specific activity that contributes to an objective to achieve a goal!

While this may all seem exceedingly mechanical, the creativity, experience, talent, and even art is in developing the mission, goals, and objectives, and in running a library by getting every employee to perform well everyday when they might rather ignore a particular task. Without the leader's talent of adapting to the ever-changing external and internal environment, any plan is useless. A good strategic plan is also a guide to direct peoples' activities when the leader is not around. We all need a vacation now and then, and a good leader knows that employees who are actively engaged in accomplishing objectives that contribute to goals can work with less frequent guidance. It is especially important in a small library with few staff to carry out activities.

Morris Chang is attributed with stating that without strategy, execution is aimless and without execution, strategy is useless. The real importance of a strategic plan is in the execution of that plan when everyone and everything is trying to head off in the direction of *business as usual* or maintaining the status quo.

Frequent Drastic Changes

The obvious next question is, "Why bother developing a strategic plan if it all depends on talent to adapt to all those changes that weren't foreseen by the plan?" In order to get where you want to be, you have to start from where you are, and without a strategic plan you don't know exactly where you are, let alone where you want to be. It's like beginning a business trip not knowing where you are leaving from or destined for; that's not going to get you anywhere! Your library's situation absolutely requires a plan because it is extremely important where you are, and critically important where you want to end up.

In the forecast portion of this 21st Century Library Strategic Plan Model, the external environment factors that you expect will impact the library's operation are included to take into account their affects. That's all you can do, evaluate, anticipate, and plan. The best you can do is carefully and honestly evaluate the conditions, both internal through strengths, weaknesses, opportunities, and threats (SWOT) analysis and external through social, technological, economic, and political (STEP) analysis, and develop your best assessment of what changes are most likely to occur in your environment during the period of the plan. Taking those into account when developing goals and objectives will better prepare your library organization for success.

Your Strategic Plan

Without an adequate strategic plan your library will likely be wasting its resources, spinning its wheels and getting nowhere. Your . . . our strategic plan should give you the roadmap to your vision of what you want your library to be. Call it anything you like, make it as detailed or general as it needs to be to meet your requirements, so that it helps you identify and get to the library that you want to offer your clientele. A thoughtful application of the recommendations in this book will give your library a really good guide to achieving your mission and vision.

PRACTICE

Library directors in any size public libraries must have good working knowledge of their strategic planning processes in order to steer the library staff, library board, stakeholders, and all participants toward accomplishing the processes and assisting in developing useful plans. If you have read this far through the justifications of why a strategic plan is important and you found yourself not totally convinced, then realize that your board and staff will be asking the same question, "Why is this important?" It is imperative before you begin the process to ensure that you have a consensus among the organization that strategic planning is an important and essential tool for success. Only then will you have the true commitment as opposed to empty agreements. True commitment will be required for participants to provide meaningful contributions to a process that will result in a useful plan with the possibility of effective implementation on all levels.

As previously mentioned, the director's knowledge of strategic planning is important for steering the process. It is important to remember that steering the organization THROUGH the process is different than steering them INTO a plan. A confident leader must accept that there will be times that the outcome of the group and committee process may produce different results than leaders would have produced on their own. It is natural to feel as the library's leader you have a firm grasp of the most important issues your library is facing. However, the process of creating a strategic plan utilizing staff, board, and stakeholders' input will logically bring issues and ideas to the front that the director must then help to incorporate into their vision for the library's future.

Also, be aware of a state of reality in which people will try to employ shortcuts at any point where they find the task too difficult or distasteful to tackle. Trust history that when participants address specific goals or objectives or activities, or any other element that fails to present an *obvious* solution, it is likely that they will look for an *easy* solution. For example, when a library uses outside consultants to conduct evaluations, or customer needs assessment, or any part of a strategic plan, staff will be quick to accept whatever they get from the consultants. This is because it's easier to rely on the recommendations of experts than to do the extra work necessary themselves to find the results they believe to be more applicable to their library.

A good example of this was in 2012 when most state library agencies conducted formal evaluations of their Five Year Library Services and Technology Act (LSTA) Plan as required by the federal agency, the Institute for Museums and Library Services (IMLS). Every five years states are required to account for how well they used the millions of dollars in federal funds received for library technology related projects. IMLS requires a formal evaluation by an unbiased third party, who can assess all the various programs that the state has conducted over the five-year period to spend the funds. Most state library agencies paid consultants to do the evaluation and provide recommendations of what initiatives the state should consider pursuing in their next Five Year LSTA Plan.

Many staff probably accepted the consultants' recommendations without even questioning, "Is that who we are? Are those the goals we want to adopt as priority initiatives? Do these recommendations further the goals we want to accomplish?" The reasons why a state might readily accept the outside consultants' recommendations are several.

(1) They paid major dollars ($50,000 or more) for the expert's recommendations.
(2) They have no better ideas because they were relying on the experts to tell them what they needed to do.
(3) They find it easier to use the recommendations they paid for than to do more work to validate the recommendations.
(4) They find it easier to use the experts' recommendations than to create their own goals, objectives, initiatives, and so forth.
(5) They have a strong desire to get through the strategic planning process and get back to work.

The point here is that every library director as leader must guard against short cuts to the process. Not until the participants have reached a satisfaction with the outcome of a particular stage or element in their strategic plan should they move on to the next. Even then the book cannot be closed on that element. Later discussions, information, and considerations may amend earlier elements of the plan. That's just the way the strategic planning process works.

DERAILMENT

Thus, it is at the very beginning where you will succeed or fail. Your commitment to create change within your library organization, your desire to create a library for the future to be relevant to a 21st Century community, your leadership to guide the planning process, and your ability to resolve conflict, which is almost guaranteed to occur will determine whether you see it through to a useful and permanent evolution from business as usual.

The proverbial "good start" is proverbial for a reason—IT'S TRUE! How you begin this strategic planning process will determine how you finish. Knowing the derailment points, being prepared for them, and what to do to resolve them will facilitate the process tremendously. Setting the tone and atmosphere for the planning process will determine how well or badly it proceeds. It may be necessary to precede the planning process with some workshops on change. Introduce a change agent into the organization and let it begin to work. Test the waters so to speak.

Do not embark on this 21st Century Library Strategic Plan Model process expecting it to be easy, or expecting there will be no change or impact to your library organization. If you try to implement the theory and practice contained in this strategic plan model, you should only do so with the intent and expectation of creating change in your library. Change is inherently difficult in organizations.

SMALL LIBRARY IDEAS

The majority of public libraries in America are small rural libraries that serve communities of less than 25,000 citizens, and have staff of less than ten full time equivalent (FTE) employees. Certainly for a library of a few employees, the group dynamics are very different from larger libraries in larger communities. In some respects running the library is less complicated, even though the challenge of doing everything with just a few staff is monumental. On the other hand, the smaller libraries are more likely to have a more tightly knit community to which they have a much closer connection. Realistically, a library of any number over about 50 employees isn't even going to get involvement and input from its entire staff.

The disadvantages are that there are fewer employees to be involved in the strategic planning process, fewer unbiased ideas, fewer perspectives to share, fewer professional experiences to bring to the process, and a tendency to conduct business more informally than larger organizations. The advantages are that library employees have a closer connection to the community, understand their customers better, can include more stakeholders from the community more intimately in the process, and more easily get community buy-in to the new strategic plan.

Obviously, making advantages out of disadvantages is the secret to developing a useful strategic plan for a small library. Each chapter in this book presents ideas for small libraries to implement the theory and practice of each topic; but to answer the question, "Why develop a strategic plan?," let it suffice for now to reiterate the same reasons that any library should have a useful plan as outlined earlier.

What library can't benefit from a staff who are being proactive rather than reactive, or communicating a common vision, manage change, and better focus activities and resources on the mission? As already stated, operations in a small library tend to be less formal, more seat-of-the-pants type activities, which when faced with limited staff resources may be a necessity. However, those are not the most desirable conditions in which to operate.

Every library staff will benefit from conducting a more formalized strategic planning process, because it forces one to answer the questions that are seldom addressed:

- What is changing within our community?
- What should our mission be? Is it still the same, or does it need to change?
- Do we have a vision? Does everyone embrace the library's vision?
- Are we meeting the needs of all our customers?
- What could we be doing more effectively?
- Are we using our limited resources as effectively as possible?
- Are we keeping up with the most current librarianship practices?

These and many more questions will be addressed if the library staff follows the strategic planning process recommended here. A director of a small library sometimes has a better opportunity to become a leader within its community to help it become a 21st Century community. Smaller libraries may be more threatened by becoming irrelevant than larger libraries. Remaining relevant to your community is the undeniable secret to survival. A thorough and useful strategic plan can help make that happen.

CHAPTER 2

The 21st Century Library Strategic Plan Model

THEORY

This chapter discusses a model 21st Century Library strategic plan. Every process requires a model from which to proceed because it will require change. Because it will require change, it will question.

Why 21st Century? In this 21st Century, much of what you thought you knew about librarianship and how to operate a library needs to be questioned. This will require you to think outside the box and ask whether you are going to accept "business as usual" or whether you are going to seek real change. It will require you to evaluate the internal and external environment in which you operate and make some estimations of the future you are going to face. Your evaluation will be based on educated credible assumptions from staff and process participants using SWOT analysis and external macro-environment STEP analysis. It may not be strategic planning as you've ever understood it before.

The Strategic Plan Process

Regardless of how extensive a process the librarian uses, the steps required to develop a useful and effective strategic plan should be followed all the way to the conclusion to ensure that the plan is indeed effective for the library's and the community's needs. Using shortcuts and skipping elements of the process will undoubtedly result in one of those typical plan documents that simply satisfy a requirement or otherwise gather dust on a shelf.

A **strategic plan** can and should be a primary management tool for the library to accomplish its **mission**. The components of this 21st Century Library Strategic Plan Model are intended to allow individuals to easily

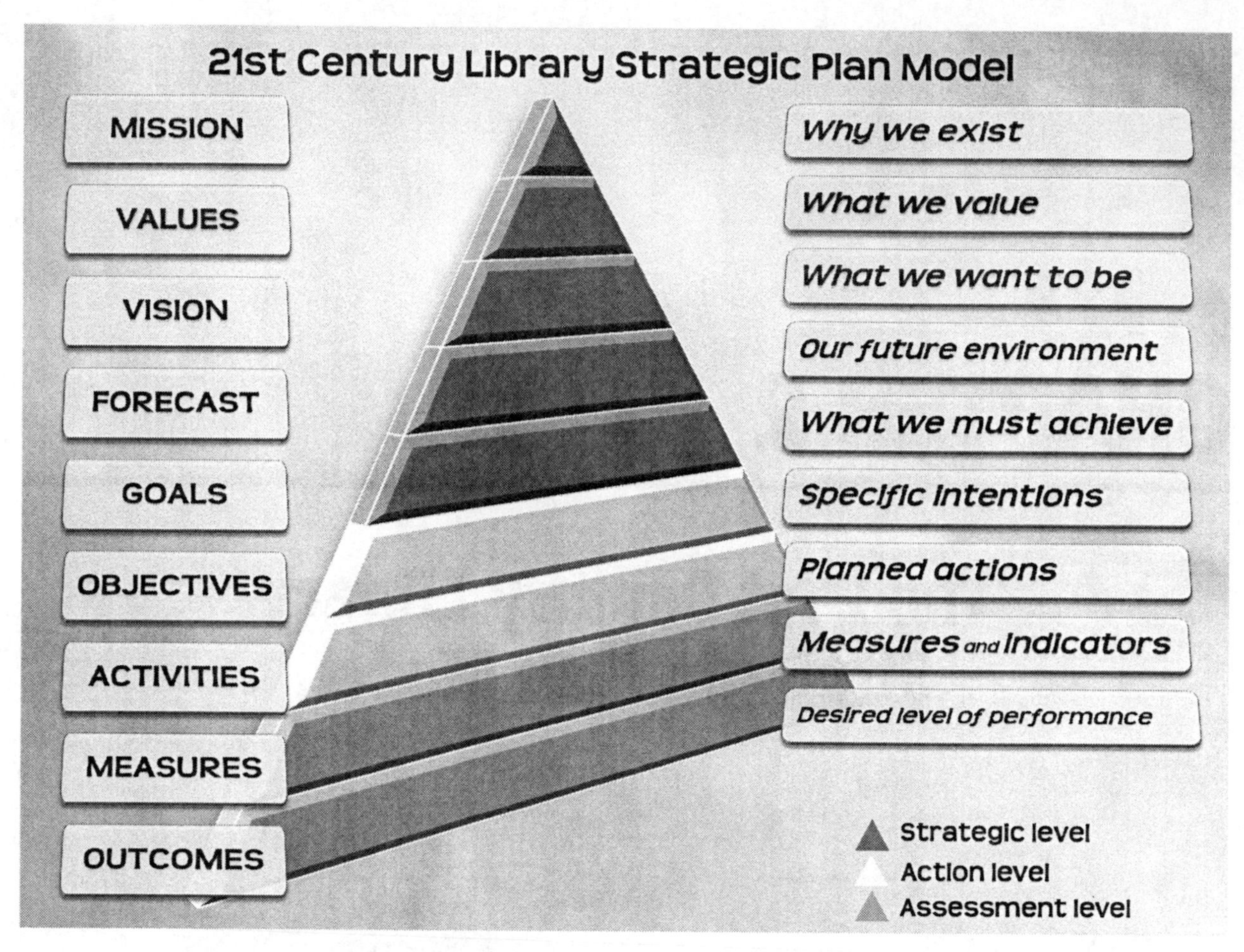

Figure 2.1 21st Century Library Strategic Plan Model

comprehend the requirements of each stage, and to follow through to their conclusion. This model comprises of the following elements (Figure 2.1).

I. **Mission Statement**—Why does YOUR library exist—not libraries in general, but YOUR library?

II. **Values and Guiding Principles**—Define and shape the organization's culture and climate, and establish the standards upon which YOUR library will operate.

III. **Vision Statement**—An image toward which the library is motivated. The vision that makes people want to be a part of YOUR library organization (Figure 2.2)

IV. **Forecast**—Understand the library's internal strengths and weaknesses and the external factors it faces in order to help guide the development of goals and objectives, and make them realistic and achievable. These address the realities of an uncertain 21st Century future and produce a means to better understand their impact.

V. **Goals**—The desired results YOU want to achieve to accomplish the mission. What more specific goals must YOU accomplish to achieve the overall mission?

VI. **Objectives**—What will YOU accomplish to achieve goals and to guide YOUR library's activities?

VII. **Activities**—YOUR library's daily, weekly, monthly, and annual functions, most of which the customer sees as the results of your activities.

VIII. **Measures and Outcomes**—The level of performance of an activity that can be determined over time using quantitative data, as well as the actual impact, benefits, and/or changes resulting from performance of YOUR activity.

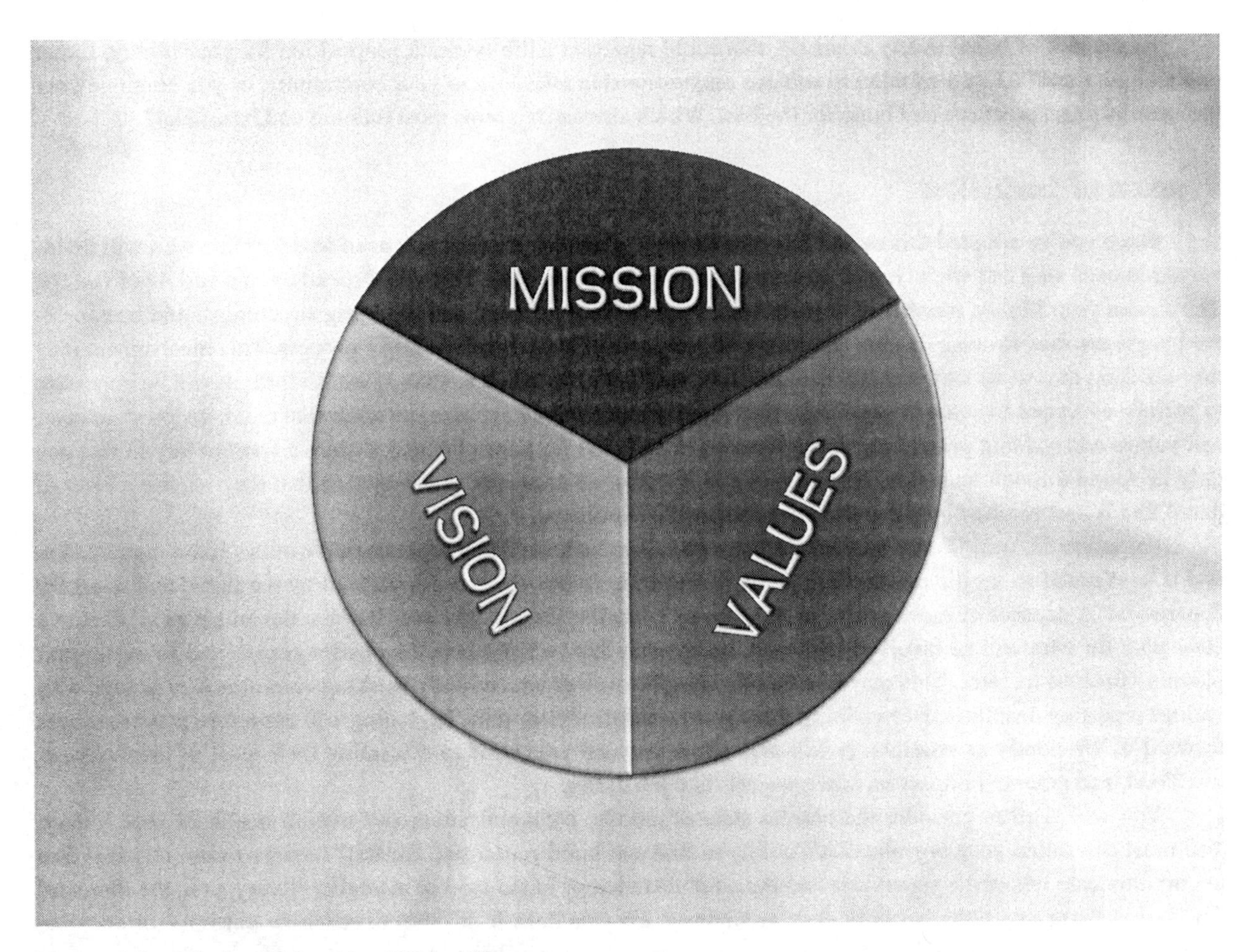

Figure 2.2 Mission, Values, and Vision Diagram

IX. **Resource Allocation**—Allocating the limited resources available to implement the activities including anything that may be used in more than one way: funds, facilities, equipment, materials, and personnel time.

X. **Appendices**—Useful ancillary documents to augment the Plan.

Appendix A—Environmental Forecast Statement
Appendix B—Broad Category Resource Allocation Chart (see Figure 10.1)
Appendix C—Detailed Resource Allocation Chart
Appendix D—Measures Collection Chart
Appendix E—Outcomes Evaluation Matrix

PRACTICE

Do you actually need to follow this model and include every step? Yes. Will you include every step? In all reality, probably not. Why? Because the process will get derailed by people's natural inclination to use shortcuts, get sidetracked, resisting change, and the natural tendency to prefer business as usual, which is exactly why serious strategic planning is not for the faint of heart. It is hard work, can take a long time, and requires dedicated library resources, but the rewards are worth the effort. It mostly depends on the leader and how dedicated they are to serious change, progress, and ensuring the library remains relevant to the community.

At the risk of being overly dramatic, this could represent a life-or-death proposition for your library. Either you and your staff adopt a mission to achieve unquestionable relevance to your community, or you continue your business as usual practices and hope for the best. Which alternative seems most rational and beneficial?

Process of Inclusion

Once you've adopted this model for your strategic planning process, you need to determine who will be involved in each step and what type of process or processes will be used. This will depend upon a variety of factors. The size of your library, number of departments, layers of management, and reporting structure should be considered to ensure that, to some degree, all levels of the organization are involved in the process. This involvement may take the form of committees, stakeholder meetings, staff polls, town hall meetings, and so forth. It will be important to include everyone to some degree in the first three components of the plan: mission statement, vision statement, and values and guiding principles. These form the foundation for your plan and require a level of buy-in that can only be found through inclusion. As you move to the other components, you may find that they require a level of detail that is best reached by a department or a specific committee.

For example, your library may have a large management team that is representative of the entire organization and is best suited to set the overarching goals, however, activities are best determined by the individual specialty department in support of those goals. In the case of a smaller library, this may involve the entire team. Create a clear plan for who will be involved with each component that includes benchmarks for completion to move your planning process forward. This may consist of a complex web of concurrently working committees or groups with various reporting deadlines. Determining these groups and deadlines at the beginning will ensure the process moves forward as efficiently as possible. It will also allow you and your staff to determine their level of involvement, workload, and potential impact on other projects and job duties.

You will need to consider the current state of morale, communication, and overall health of your library. You must determine your organization's ability to find and build consensus. Do staff members currently feel free to communicate with their supervisor and the administration or in the case of a smaller library, you, the director? Answering these questions is rarely easy and often a director finds it difficult to reach an objective or accurate diagnosis. Therefore, discussing the issue openly at the initial stages of your planning process is a key to success. Open communication is an indispensable component of the planning process.

Planning for the future requires understanding where you are today. Often this understanding is only found through a critical look at current processes, services, staffing, and structures to determine the areas with challenges and need for improvement. Staff must feel comfortable sharing their ideas on the current state of the library, the future, the challenges, and the changes that they believe are important to continue moving toward the future. Throughout the planning process the director must continue to reassure all levels of staff that honest and open communication is necessary, desired, and will be accepted without judgment or retaliation.

Additional Benefits

One of the most important reasons to create a strategic plan is to create an organization and culture of empowerment and inclusion. A well-designed plan with detailed objectives and activities allows all members of your organization to lead from any position because they know where the organization is headed. They are able to create viable input and make informed decisions within the scope of their various positions in the organization, which will help drive the organization toward the mission and the vision.

This common understanding provides important benefits. It creates a spirit of inclusion that increases staff morale. No one can argue the importance of this characteristic to a successful organization. It creates an empowered staff that is able to dynamically respond to situations as they arise whether in customer service, committee work, or individual daily decision-making, which improves every aspect of your organization. Creating a plan that outlines a roadmap to the organization's goals enables the entire staff to be working WITH the leadership of the organization not following blinding. It is always easier to move forward as a group sharing a common understanding of the mission and the vision, than to drag or push others toward the goals and objectives.

Strong leaders can utilize not only the resulting plan but also the planning process to strengthen and improve their library. Every process step and assignment will create stronger lines of communication and trust at all levels within your organization.

DERAILMENT

Deciding to use the 21st Century Library Strategic Plan Model can facilitate the planning process and upgrade your chances of developing a useful plan. However, being intimately familiar with the stages of the model, the requirements of the process, and the practical aspects of implementing the process will further help ensure a successful outcome. Also, being familiar with derailment points will help you be prepared for them and facilitate keeping participants on track and productive. The last thing you want is a discouraged group wasting their time dwelling on unproductive issues and ending up shortcutting the process.

The worst possible thing you can face at this beginning is a group of individuals who only want to *get through this and get back to work.* That attitude will ensure that people are closed-minded, seeking shortcuts wherever they can find them and hoping to avoid change at almost any cost.

If you—the library director—*are* interested in change, this process will facilitate it. If you are *not* interested in real change, then this process will not cause it.

Deciding on the best person within your organization to accomplish the strategic planning task is extremely important. If you are determined to create change within your library, ensure that the most passionate and capable person in your organization leads the task, or committee, or team, whether that's you or someone else. If you are undecided about change in your organization, but you want to develop the best plan possible, assign a capable person to head the strategic planning task and watch what happens. If you do not want change in your library but have a requirement to develop a better plan than the one you have now, adopt the 21st Century Library Strategic Plan Model, assign the task to someone who is capable of both leading the team but capable of doing it the way you ask them to do it. Let them do the work required to adopt the new plan making it clear to them what you prefer and want, which is not to make drastic changes at this point in your organization's development, and let them do a much shorter process with a few staff members who will be agreeable with what you want to put forward at this time. It's your library. It's your choice.

This 21st Century Library Strategic Plan Model is offered as a process to create change. It is all about eliminating "business as usual." The intention of this 21st Century Library Strategic Plan Model is to facilitate the improvements in your library's mission, vision, and goals, provide a plan with focus, and develop effective activities, all to enable your library to remain relevant to your community in the 21st Century.

SMALL LIBRARY IDEAS

In a small library, where you have a staff of less than 10 FTE, it is difficult at best to get everyone together at the same time and to share a wide diversity of education, background, experience, and opinion. Your resources are drastically limited to very few hours each week for planning. This process can work for your library as well, but there may need to be some alternatives for it to work best for your circumstances.

Look around at what other stakeholders are available to help. Consider asking trustees, friends of the library members, community leaders, government officials, and the community in general for participation. All have a vested interest in making the library the best it can be. That deepens the list of people who might be willing to help.

Unfortunately, bringing in others from outside the organization may require the director to be willing to give up a certain amount of control. The director must be confident in their ability to facilitate the process BEFORE getting these stakeholders involved. Once you've received outside participation in the process, it can easily move in directions that are unproductive and potentially divisive. In most cases, the people identified here are Type

A personalities, that is, leaders. Getting too many leaders and not enough followers involved in your strategic plan process could be the first potential derailment point.

Let's assume that you have a cooperative and capable group of supporters and community that you think will follow your facilitation efforts, so you get them involved. What's the first thing you do? Conduct training on the strategic plan process. Have an initial organizational meeting where you lay out the goals of the strategic plan process, identify your expectations of the group, and discuss the details of the stages involved in the strategic plan process. You will also want to establish timelines for completion of each stage, identify the results of each stage, and ensure the individual buy-in of every member of your team.

This process has some remarkable benefits for your library. It can help people understand the complexities you face in running the library because they will get an intimate perspective they never knew before. It will also allow these supporters to feel greater ownership in their community library. People in small communities tend to feel like that anyway, but this will focus that support and interest on your library. This diverse group of individuals from the community will bring new perspectives to your library operations: business perspectives, parent perspectives, resident perspectives, and maybe even new library customer perspectives. Allowing this group to see your vision for their library is the beginning to making it happen.

CHAPTER 3

Mission Statement

THEORY

Consider the question, "How do you get from where your library is now to become a 21st Century Library?" The simple answer is, "Develop a strategy based on the 21st Century Library Strategic Plan Model offered here." This chapter lays the foundation for YOU to begin to answer that question.

Mission

This strategic plan model begins with the **mission statement** because the reason why you exist should come before everything else, even the **vision**. Without the parameters defined by a mission, the vision could be anything, which might not even directly relate to your library, let alone be realistic.

It also needs to be understood that the mission, vision, and values statements work in concert to create a complete definition of your library. Therefore, it is highly useful to exploit the unique purposes of each of the three statements rather than try to make each statement independently define your library (Figure 3.1).

Mission Statement Template

Recognizing that a generic strategic plan resembles a generic train wreck in that it has so many variables that it is hard to describe in a generic way, it really requires some particulars to make it meaningful. However, consider the following.

"The _______ (*passenger, tourist, grain, coal, auto carrier, or tanker car*) train was traveling toward _______ (*Minneapolis, Kansas City, Durango, or New Orleans*) when it collided with a _______ (*cow, automobile, avalanche, or train*) causing it to _______ (*be delayed, kill the cow, derail, demolish two miles of track, or burst into flames*)."

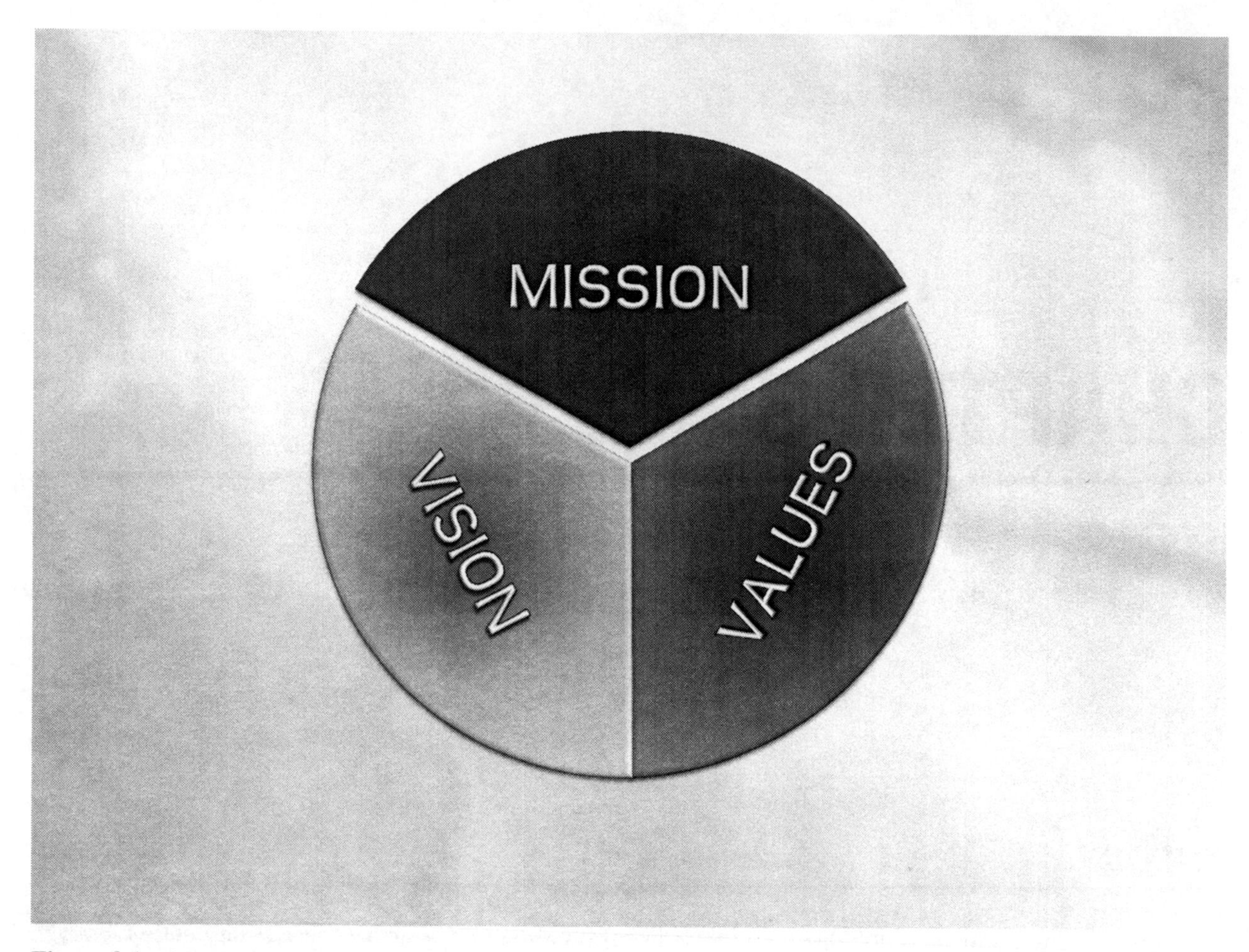

Figure 3.1 Mission, Values, and Vision Diagram

As the earlier narrative demonstrates, one can use a template for a mission statement to include certain useful elements of the statement. It is not essential, but certainly helpful. The following is a good template for a library mission statement that puts it together in a coherent flow.

- Name,
- intent to do,
- what,
- how,
- in order to achieve, and
- (other elements if you feel the need)

In order to be a useful mission statement, it must be realistic and achievable. What is the library's mission in the 21st Century? Is it different from or the same as it has always been? Many believe it is the same because it is a "core" mission (*whatever that means in a 21st Century context*). The fact that real-world libraries are changing to survive supports the assertion that any core mission that existed has changed to address the environmental changes that have occurred in the 21st Century (Figure 3.2).

Why does YOUR library exist? Most libraries exist for a more specific purpose than to pursue a generic mission. For example—*Develop, promote, and improve library and information services in order to ensure access*

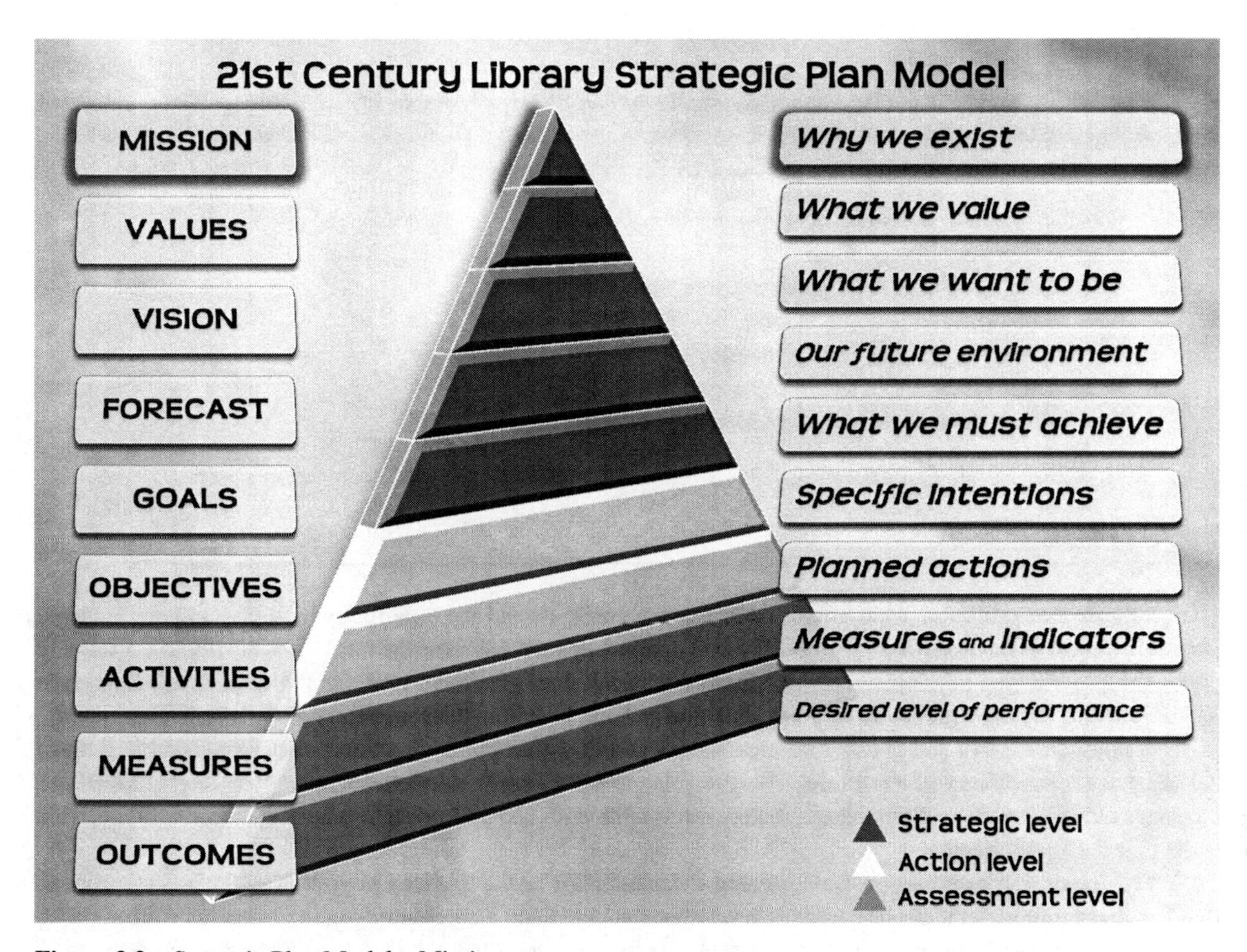

Figure 3.2 Strategic Plan Model—Mission

to information for all—is so generic as to make it almost useless in providing any direction or parameters for the remaining elements of the strategic plan. What goals and objectives would you develop from a mission statement like this? What kind of useful strategic plan would that create for your future library? Why not use the same old tired ones you've always used?

It is hard to imagine a library mission statement that can be both 100 years old and yet have enough flexibility and comprehension to include the many societal factors that have influenced public libraries for over a century. It would be very unlikely that the statement would be still relevant today. You would ask yourself if this mission is still appropriate for a 21st Century Library. It is a decision that the library director and staff, the library board, and community must make even if the mission statement remains static for decades. If the mission statement allows your plan to incorporate the 21st Century goals, objectives, and activities that employ 21st Century librarianship techniques that are appropriate and necessary, then it can work for your library.

Even if your plan appears to achieve a good meld between the old and the new for your community and appears to be a strategic plan that works for your library and community, is it a 21st Century Library strategic plan? Will it achieve a 21st Century Library goal that your community and library need to not only survive, but also thrive in a 21st Century world? (Verma, 2009).

The Statement

Whether the library is public, school, academic, or special has a huge impact on your statement. However, there are some recommended elements of any mission statement that you may want to review before reconsidering your own mission statement. A mission statement could contain language to:

- provide a general statement of why your library exists;
- clarify what your library does;
- capture the essence of what you want your library to achieve;
- have some measurable components;
- be short and simple enough to remember;
- be an action statement in active voice; and
- be a living statement subject to revision as your needs require.

PRACTICE

So now that you know what a mission statement should be and the vital role it will play in your strategic plan, it is time to get started making yours. The first derailment point concerns the fact that many librarians actually prefer the generic type mission statement, simply because it does give them total flexibility in developing goals and objectives. They can go in virtually any direction and still be within the parameters of the mission statement.

A more descriptive and focused mission statement will define which direction you need to head to achieve the mission of your library of the future. If you're going to use a generic mission statement, you might as well use the same old tired goals and objectives you're comfortable with and end up right where you currently are. This is the first deadly shortcut.

The creation of your best possible mission statement must be the first step in your overall planning process. Bearing that in mind, let's discuss creating a mission statement and also group dynamic issues as well. As with other phases in the strategic planning process, there are two key steps that will lead to a successful outcome:

- determining where you are now and
- building consensus.

Determining Where You Are Now

First and foremost, throughout most of the strategic planning process you will repeatedly find yourself assessing, "Where are we now?" and "Where are we starting?" This will determine everything that comes after. In the mission statement creation phase, this is a fairly easy question to answer. The answer will come easily: "We have a really good mission statement" or "We do not have a relevant mission statement."

So, if you all agree that you have a really good mission statement, the next question is simple, "Is it still working for us?" If the answer is "Yes," and you are sure of the answer, then rejoice and move on. Do not just hurry through this decision to move on to the next phase. This is the foundation for the process yet to come.

If the answer is no, not really, maybe, or any other form of apathetic response, then you have either of the following two choices:

(1) Tweak what you have, which is always a risky business as you may either refine it to perfection or absolute mush.
(2) Throw it out and re-answer the first question, "We do not have a good mission statement."

The choice is yours and how bonded your organization is to the current mission statement.

If you originally answered that you do not have a useful mission statement or have now determined that the one you have is no longer viable, you need to create your statement. This means it's time to move to the next step, building consensus. *See, you're on your way!*

Building Consensus

This will be the first opportunity you have in your strategic planning process to work on this very important step. Writing a brief mission statement should be fairly simple compared to an entire plan, so, you should use this opportunity as manager of this planning process to determine your organization's or committee's or team's ability to find and build consensus.

Therefore, in an effort to not only create the mission statement, but also to determine your group's level of consensus-building ability, throw them in the deep end of the pool. Make the mission statement creation the first agenda item at your first meeting. Throw it out there. "We have determined we need a (new, better, relevant, foresighted, visionary, etc.) mission statement. What do we want it to be?" Now is where you will see what type of group you have to work with. Will they begin brainstorming immediately, sit silently, defer to the highest ranking person in the room, dissect the bits the first suggestion offered, or let the first idea frame the rest of the ideas and conversation?

At this point, your leadership skills will be necessary to either encourage or discourage the healthy and productive or destructive habits of your group. As you progress, remember an example from nature, the skilled and intelligent border collie who can guide a herd (*yes, that term works for this point*) not by pushing from behind or running out in front, but rather by constant and steady circling and intense observation. If you keep that example in mind, you will successfully guide your group. You will not find yourself pushing them in one direction or another; thereby sabotaging the organic creation of ideas bigger than any one individual. You will also create an environment where consensus builds naturally because no individual feels trampled or unheard, but rather a part of the process.

As you learn the dynamics of your group, you must still remember that the goal of this particular discussion for the group is the successful creation of a mission statement. So guide them with simple nudges. Continue to remind them of the basics of what a mission statement should be as outlined earlier in this chapter. Finally, when you see their ideas starting to coalesce, help your group to conclude their process by affirming when a successful outcome has been achieved. This may sound obvious but think of your experiences in committee work and the times you have looked around at the whole and thought, "Are we done? Did we do it?"

As the leader of your group, it is up to you to know when the goal has been reached and convey that to the whole, or recognize when you have reached the group's limit of productivity. You must also be able to decide when further work would be less productive than the group has already produced and stop. Don't let the group become discouraged at this early stage by unproductive work.

Organizational Influences

Again, a mission statement has many reality constraints due to external influences and often mission requirements prescribed by someone else. In many library organizations the higher level agency, whether local government jurisdiction, governing board, benefactors, or statutes and ordinances, sometimes dictates a prescribed mission in more or less detail. These mission requirements must be taken into consideration when developing the mission statement, and it may be very difficult guiding the group toward selecting any alternatives.

One alternative to trying to incorporate these requirements into a mission statement is to reserve the mission requirement language for goals. As long as the prescribed mission requirements are contained in the strategic plan, there may be no rule that requires them to be a part of the mission statement. (*Again, the only requirement for this rule is whatever works for your library.*) Under prescribed circumstances it might be more beneficial to develop a mission statement that is brief, broad in scope, and, perhaps, something like a motto.

21st Century Library Example

The National Library Service for the Blind and Physically Handicapped of The Library of Congress, has a very simple Mission Statement, "That All May Read . . . " (NLS, 2012). It is simple, straight forward, memorable, even poignant, and somewhat inspiring. Topeka & Shawnee County Public Library has a more modern library Mission Statement that reads: "Your place. Stories you want. Information you need. Connections you seek" (Topeka & Shawnee County (KS) Public Library, 2012). If your library is constrained by prescribed mission requirements, or simply interested in developing a mission statement that even your customers and stakeholders can remember, consider a short one.

Hopefully, you get the idea that there is no useful generic library mission statement. Are you wondering if your authors can offer an example of a 21st Century Library mission statement? Here it goes.

Mission Statement

"The Xxxxxx Library will fulfill the 21st Century learning, recreational, and literary needs of the Xxxxx Community through service that exceeds expectations in physical and virtual environments that promote a literate community and enhance every residents' quality of life."

Assessment

Although only a simple sample, it does contain many of the elements that would make it a useful mission statement. It is active voice, states why our library exists and what it does, is relatively short and simple, and provides some measurable components from which goals and objectives can be created. It includes recognition that our library will satisfy "21st Century learning, recreational, and literary needs," which has a whole connotation apart from simply providing business as usual library services, and it also makes reference to virtual environments. Satisfying needs through service that exceeds expectations includes a context for using 21st Century technology to accomplish that, as well as reference services that satisfy the needs of the 21st Century customers or patrons. These contexts and explanations of the mission statement's full meaning can be included in subsequent sections of the strategic plan through the goals and objectives.

DERAILMENT

In any planning process progress may be delayed with derailment tactics. The biggest derailment factor at this point is simply resistance to change. People individually and in organizations are naturally resistant to change because it usually causes them to get outside their comfort zone, address issues they prefer not to address, consider different ways of doing things, and in general, having to alter the way they work. Strategic planning is already outside most peoples' comfort zones because they are being asked to look into the future and make decisions about how they will operate in that future, often revising or even discarding activities they have been accomplishing seemingly successfully over short and long term.

Expecting librarians and library workers to reconsider their mission is like telling them everything they thought they knew about librarianship is now obsolete. That's their initial reaction. However, reassessing the way one does one's job and carries out one's business is not saying that what one has been doing is wrong. It's just that some activities are no longer as productive or effective as they once were. Business as usual within the library world will not guarantee that the library will remain relevant to the community when all around your community, your customers, your and their technology, and society in general, is involved in frequent, even constant change. Business as usual is not a rational approach, and ignoring the need to accept change is a recipe for a steady decline. You need to be ready for this resistance.

The first sign of trouble will come when someone says to their colleagues or subordinates, "Don't worry. This won't change the way you do business." That is a huge red flag that the person who made that statement plans to retain a business as usual posture. This person will avoid getting anyone from their colleagues to their subordinates disrupted by anything even hinting of change. The leader must take that person aside and help them understand, "This process is all about change, and you can either participate and manage the change for yourself and others or we will need to do it for you." There can be no misunderstanding on this point. If you as leader truly want to implement change and progress in the organization, then people need to accept that there will be change.

Change is necessary. Change needs to be managed toward progress. We all know the old adage. Not all change is progress. And it is true. However, our job as librarians in this new environment is to make sure this change is progress. The best way to do that as an organization means accomplishing this with collaboration and consensus in mapping a new direction.

SMALL LIBRARY IDEAS

"This appears to be too involved for my small library." This would be a very natural reaction. Similarly, this is the biggest complaint given about Sandra Nelson's *Strategic Planning for Results* (Nelson, 2008), that the long-range planning process is too complicated. That and the 18 service responses with a smorgasbord of traditional library missions are all made for a very rote process that even librarians in many larger libraries have a difficult time accomplishing. It is entirely possible that your library may never have had a useful mission statement. This will be your chance to create one.

This 21st Century Library Strategic Plan Model strips the process to the bare bones and provides a structured process that any library can implement. However, the director of a small library may find that not everything in this book is appropriate for their organization. How they go about accomplishing the various elements will be somewhat different. Frankly, every library's process is different, regardless of the size of the organization. That's the nature of organizations, they all operate differently.

As stated in the previous chapter, a small library with minimal staff may want to include more stakeholders in its process and include customers, community activists, school librarians, local politicians, friends of the library group members, and so on. You may find it advantageous to include both the outspoken and connected stakeholders for advocacy purposes. However you go about it, developing a mission statement that reflects why you exist, why your library is relevant to your community, why you need community support, and why your employees come to work every morning, is equally as important to you as it is to any size library, for exactly the same reasons.

Your mission is neither related to nor dependent upon your library size. Your mission depends on your vision, your ideals, and your dreams for your library in response to the questions given earlier. Your mission statement will establish the foundation from which you can build all of the elements of any strategic plan. If you want to use the same mission statement you've always used, odds are you'll end up with the same kind of plan that will sit on the shelf and collect dust. If you recognize a bigger future for your library, you'll develop a mission statement that reflects that, from which you'll begin to build a better vision for your library's future, adopt goals that will enlarge your capabilities, and establish objectives that will lead to success.

It may seem an insurmountable task if you do not have a mission statement or you are hesitant to revise your statement. As stated earlier, mission statements can be borrowed from many sources, library organizations, as well as other types of organizations. You do not have to reinvent the wheel, or make the process more difficult than it has to be. Use the examples you find everywhere and get involvement from your stakeholders.

Whether big or small library—the process for committee work and idea creation may change as indicated in Chapter 1, but the mission statement itself is more about your community's and organization's culture and future than your size. You should understand your community, board, and organization better than anyone, so follow your instincts and get those involved who can help the most.

CHAPTER 4

Values and Guiding Principles

THEORY

The **values** statement, which often includes **guiding principles**, along with mission and vision statements, defines an organization's culture and climate, and establishes the standards upon which it operates. It also establishes for every employee those values against which their performance may be measured along with the organization's performance, as well as some standards for describing the path toward the library's success. The values statement is about who you are, your character, as compared to the mission statement that declares why you exist, and the vision statement that declares who you want to be (see Figure 4.1 on page 22).

The reason to place the values and guiding principles step after the mission and before the vision is to provide further clarity to why the organization exists by elaborating on what the organization is, in order to frame a better concept upon which to build the vision. Since the vision is the final element of the overall concept for defining your library, it will complete that description by allowing the three elements to form a synergy among the three statements, which is a good reason to make all the three statements short enough to be memorable (see Figure 4.2 on page 23).

Every organization should be guided by a set of values. Values should not change significantly, unless something drastically changes the organization, but often these require clarification, and even re-clarification to resonate with the organizational culture.

- Values provide an underlying framework for making decisions, which is part of the organization's culture.
- Values are often rooted in ethical themes, such as equality, honesty, trust, integrity, respect, fairness, and social and environmental consciousness.
- Values should be applicable across the entire organization.
- Values express who you are as an organization.
- Values provide a set of expectations for conduct that helps to shape the organizational culture.

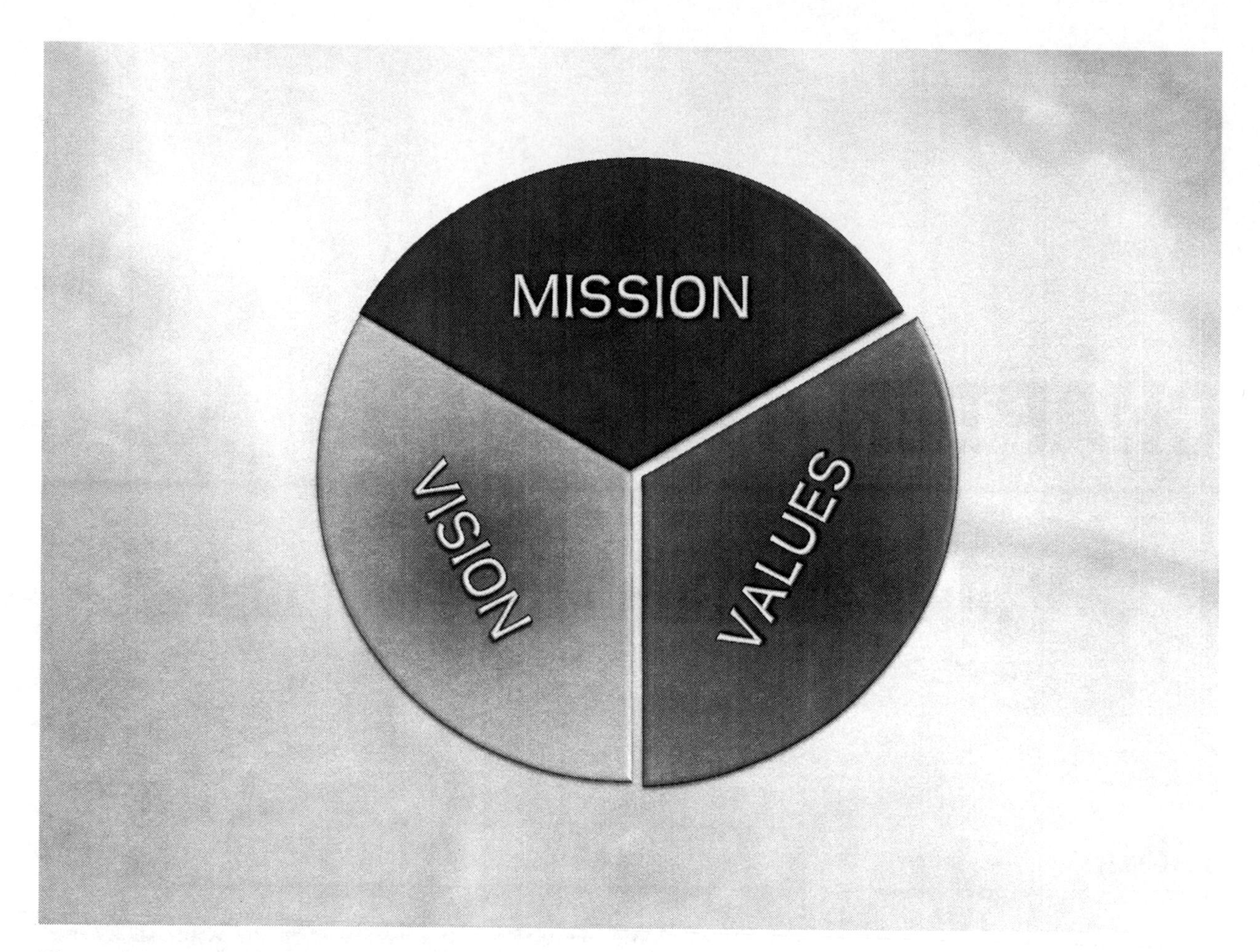

Figure 4.1 Mission, Values, and Vision Diagram

Values and Guiding Principles Descriptors

When developing these statements it is often helpful to have some action words that help people to visualize what kinds of words, or in this case values, communicate the ideas intended. Figure 4.3 (see page 24) is a set of descriptive words appropriate for developing a Values and Guiding Principles Statement.

PRACTICE

One of the most difficult tasks in the strategic planning process is to keep staff actively engaged in the process. In some stages throughout the process staff engagement will vary from a lack of interest to wariness to sometimes downright defensiveness. The lack of interest can be easily understood. It comes in the form of thoughts or statements such as "What does this have to do with me?," "How long is this planning thing going to take?," "Wouldn't it be better to just let *[somebody]* DO IT?," or the often heard, "I have work to do back at my desk!" Wariness and defensiveness will be discussed later in this book as they become more prone to occur at the later parts of the process. At this stage of planning, you are likely to find staff experiencing a lack of interest.

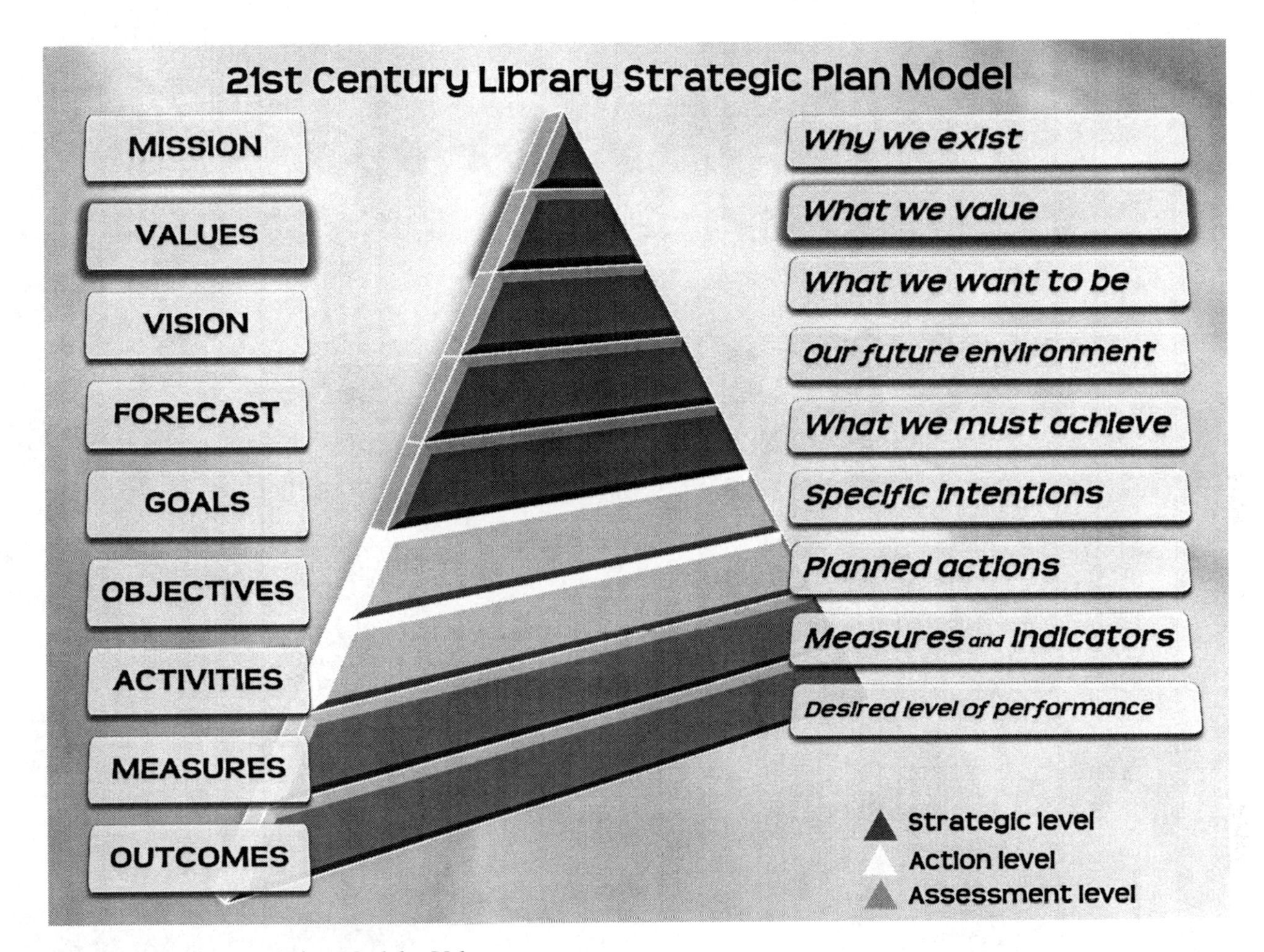

Figure 4.2 Strategic Plan Model—Values

The values and guiding principles discussion is a perfect time to draw staff back into the planning. The passion of your leadership and commitment will also be a key component in success. How passionate are you about **who** you are as an organization?

Many times new staff, after the training and orientation and some time on the job, still make decisions or engage in actions that leave you asking, "Didn't we train this person?" The answer is, in all likelihood, "Yes, you did." Your new staff members were trained on tasks, process, responsibilities, and structure—the "hows" of their job. But were they trained on the "whys"? Training often details the process used in dealing with patron records, but not the whys or the values behind the process. As long-time staff or professionals know, there are library codes of ethics and patron privacy policies that guide the processes and actions. However, for new staff and sometimes long-time staff, too, it is vital to truly explain the values behind these codes and policies. In doing so, you give staff the ability to think critically about their actions rather than simply a set of steps for finishing a process.

Values and guiding principles are key. These are the statements and guideposts you can provide to new staff to help them understand the **who** of the organization to which they now belong. As you approach this step in the planning process, explain this concept to staff. The opportunity to participate in the creation of this portion of the document, to detail what the members of your organization believe in, what they prize, and what they value most dearly about **who** you are and why you do what you do, should be exciting and revitalizing to staff if framed correctly (Pells, 2012).

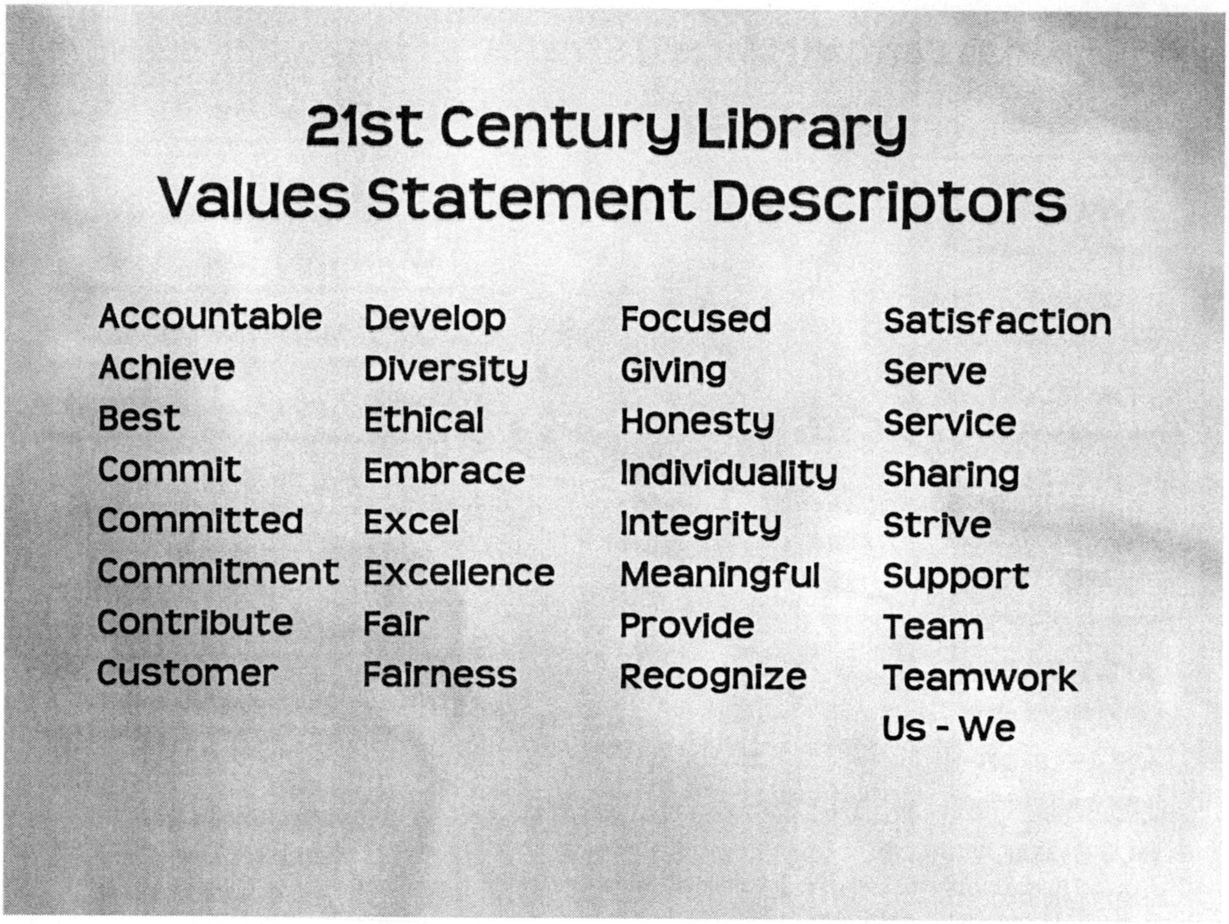

21st Century Library
Values Statement Descriptors

Accountable	Develop	Focused	Satisfaction
Achieve	Diversity	Giving	Serve
Best	Ethical	Honesty	Service
Commit	Embrace	Individuality	Sharing
Committed	Excel	Integrity	Strive
Commitment	Excellence	Meaningful	Support
Contribute	Fair	Provide	Team
Customer	Fairness	Recognize	Teamwork
			Us - We

Figure 4.3 Values Statement Descriptors

As you begin this part of the process, remind yourself and the group that these statements are about the best of **who** you are as an organization. You will include statements that detail who you are now, as well as who you are working to become. This is the time to recommit to areas the group feels need added emphasis. If your organization has received criticism for something either through the press, word of mouth, comment cards, or internally, now is the time to reaffirm your commitment or clarify the organization's value system.

Examples

If you have had a difficult audit with findings of ineffective cash accountability, you may include a value concerning the responsible use of public funds. If your community has specific concerns about an issue, for example, children accessing inappropriate Internet content, you may clarify your position. This is where these values tell the world **who** your organization is. If your organization filters the Internet your statement might be: "We believe in providing a safe cyber environment for youth through the use of filters and other software technologies." If you do not filter the content in your library and instead feel that children should be monitored by their parents or guardians, then your statement might be: "We believe that parents/guardians are the only appropriate monitors of their children's access to technology and information. We support a parent's/guardian's right to determine the appropriateness of specific content for their child as determined by their value system." You see how each of those statements speaks to the same issue but comes from very different value systems. That is how a value statement tells the community, your staff, and the world **who** your organization is and what its staff believes.

This part of the process can be passionate as you explore professional philosophies and commitments to issues such as censorship, patron privacy, or access to information. It can also be healing as you look closely at areas in which your staff members have found themselves lacking, such as managerial communication, commitment to diversity, or creating open dialogs within the community. These are merely examples. Your library is unique and will therefore have a unique set of issues that you will find require emphasis, improvement, or recommitment.

A Sample Statement

"The Xxxxxx Library values free public access to information resources collected to satisfy all segments of the Xxxxxx Community, provided through exceptionally personal and innovative public service.

Xxxxxx Library Guiding Principles:

- We serve every patron's information needs with courteous, knowledgeable, and superior staff interactions, and intelligent collection design.
- We recognize every adult's right to uncensored information within the bounds of established laws, and strive to provide requested access in as many formats as practical.
- We strive for superior quality in all library services and programs.
- We recognize and respect diversity of cultures, thinking, literacy, learning styles, age, background, and talents.
- We foster an open communication work environment to embrace honesty, integrity, professional ethics, and accountability.
- We strive to achieve courtesy and respect in all of our working relationships, both internal and external.
- We recognize the value of rapidly changing technological, economic, political, and social environments, and strive to incorporate them as much as possible and appropriate into our library culture and operations."

Assessment

Having provided a basis for values statements, most of the examples you'll encounter do not address anything specifically of 21st Century as this sample does. But, should they? Is the definition of values and principles a timeless thing? Has integrity or honesty or excellence changed in some way because of 21st Century influences? Those are questions for you to answer.

This sample has incorporated some 21st Century elements into the guiding principles, because that is an appropriate place to establish that your library does recognize the importance of "rapidly changing technological, economic, political, and social environments" and their impact on the library, as well as the library's commitment to address them and "strive to incorporate as much as possible and appropriate into our library culture." We cannot be oblivious to these 21st Century influences in our libraries, and we must try to embrace them as library services evolve to meet the 21st Century information consumers need.

DERAILMENT

The Values and Guiding Principles Statement can be a major derailment point. People normally have strong feelings about values. In many organizations there is usually someone with bad feelings toward the organization or other people in it. Some people feel they may have been marginalized, insulted, passed over for promotions or attractive assignments, or in some way treated unfairly by those in management positions. Therefore, their personal agendas will surface in discussions of values and guiding principles. They will want to ensure that the organization operates more fairly in the future, and guards against the kind of treatment they experienced.

Whether their grievance is legitimate or not, a perceived problem is as real as a similar real problem. You must be ready to deal with the personal issues that surface during discussions of organizational values. If the leader is already aware of such problems, they might want to intercede with the individuals involved and prevent a major issue from surfacing. That is not to say that any issues should be suppressed, but simply that they should be resolved before they enter the public forum and become more complicated than necessary.

SMALL LIBRARY IDEAS

Are values or guiding principles different for small libraries or any other type of library for that matter? The answer should be a resounding "No." Values and guiding principles are essentially universal to every organization, whether an organization has formalized them or not. The only challenge for any librarian is that there are so many possible ones from which to choose and decide what values and guiding principles for your library to define **who** it is.

The examples and samples included in this chapter are as applicable to a small library as to any library. One difference you may find is that your small library may include more members of the community in your core group. This will create a different dynamic for values in that you may find a smaller emphasis on professional issues such as patron privacy, ethics, censorship, and so forth. This is certainly not due to any lack of concern for these issues among the community but rather the simple fact that they are inherently librarianship issues that may not come to the forefront in a group made primarily of nonlibrarians. As such, you will want to continue to insert these ideas into the discussion in a more deliberate manner. Remember, the values and guiding principles speak to the core of **who** your library is, and they are best found in bedrock of solid professional ideals.

CHAPTER 5

Vision Statement

THEORY

Probably the most troublesome aspect of the **vision statement** is how it differs from the mission statement. If you review very many you will find elements of both intermingled with each other because it is difficult for some to separate the mission from the vision. Where the mission statement addresses the question of "Why does my library exist?," the vision statement presents an image toward which the library staff is motivated and inspires a compelling future, what they want the library to become, something more than it has been in years past and to be more than some thought it could be (Figure 5.1).

A definition which is particularly appropriate in this context is "vision is a mental image produced by the imagination." What will you dare to dream that your library can become in this 21st Century environment? Whatever it is, **dream it!** And make it your vision statement (Lucas, 1998).

The reason the vision statement comes at this point in the process is because you have developed some parameters within which you can develop your vision that will make it realistic, achievable, and relevant to your library. If you began with the vision, you might not have a firm foundation of your mission around which you can develop a vision, and the vision might be so fantastic or seemingly unrealistic that it would be useless, seen by some as ridiculously unachievable or by others as highly inappropriate (Figure 5.2).

Keep in mind that this vision does not include any assumption that you have a total understanding of the future, the 21st Century environment that will influence your library's future. Regardless of what the future looks like tomorrow or next year, your vision is what you want to become. Working to overcome or capitalize on the future is part of your strategy to implement your plan. What you want the library's 21st Century future to be is also an

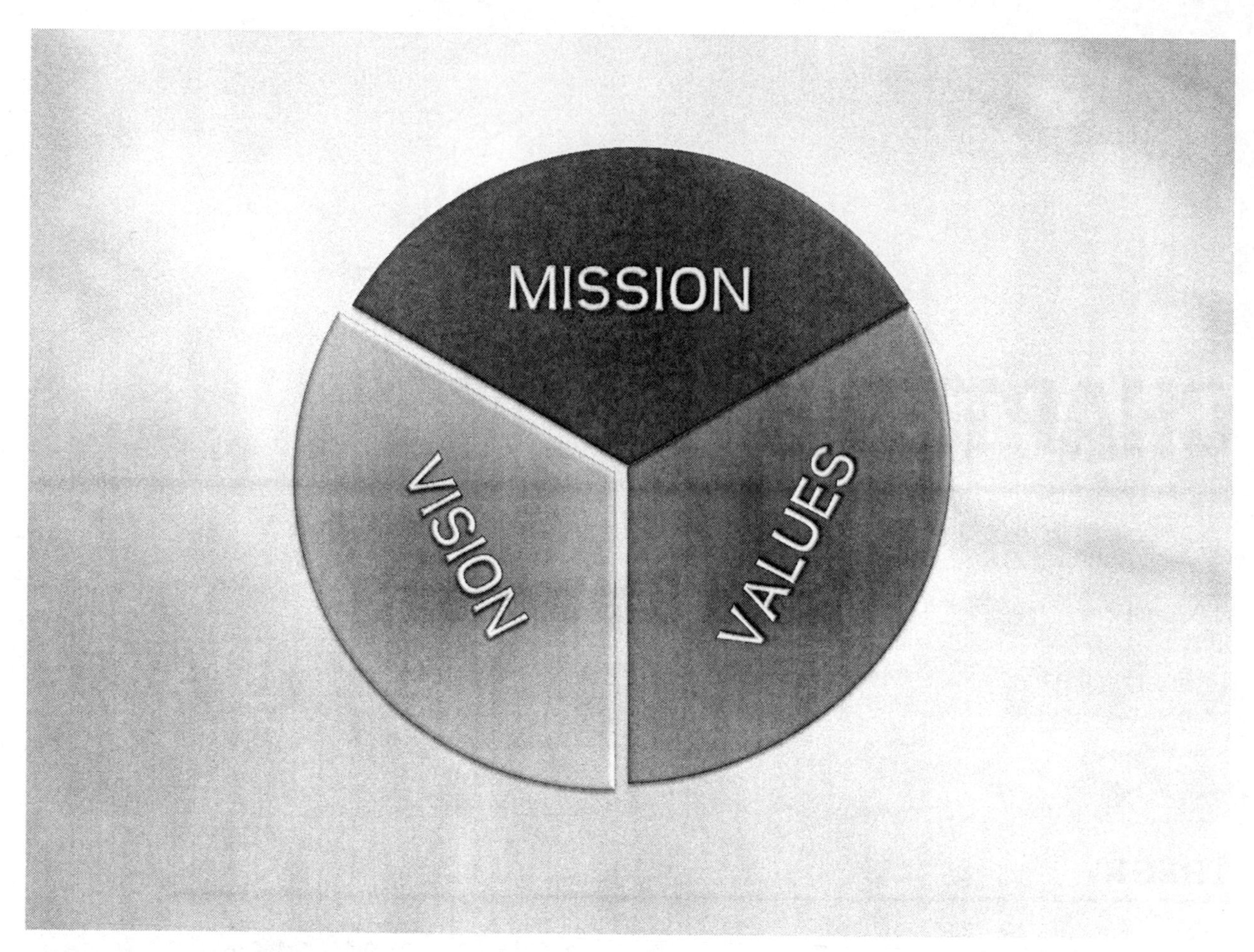

Figure 5.1 Mission, Values, and Vision Diagram

important decision, but the questions and uncertainties of the future should not constrain your vision to the point that it is not visionary and inspiring (Brown, 1998).

Vision

Like the mission statement, there is no generic library vision statement. Whether the library is public, school, academic, or special has a huge impact on your vision of what you want to become. Recommended elements of a vision statement that you may want to review when developing your own vision for the 21st Century Library include the following:

- Be an image toward which the library is motivated, guided by the strategic plan.
- Challenge everyone to reach for something significant inspiring a compelling future that is achievable.
- Be an expression of how you want your library to be perceived in the future, what success looks like.
- Provide a long-term focus for the entire library.
- Include a vivid description of the library as its operations are effectively carried out.
- Be library culture specific.
- Be the most enjoyable part of a plan.

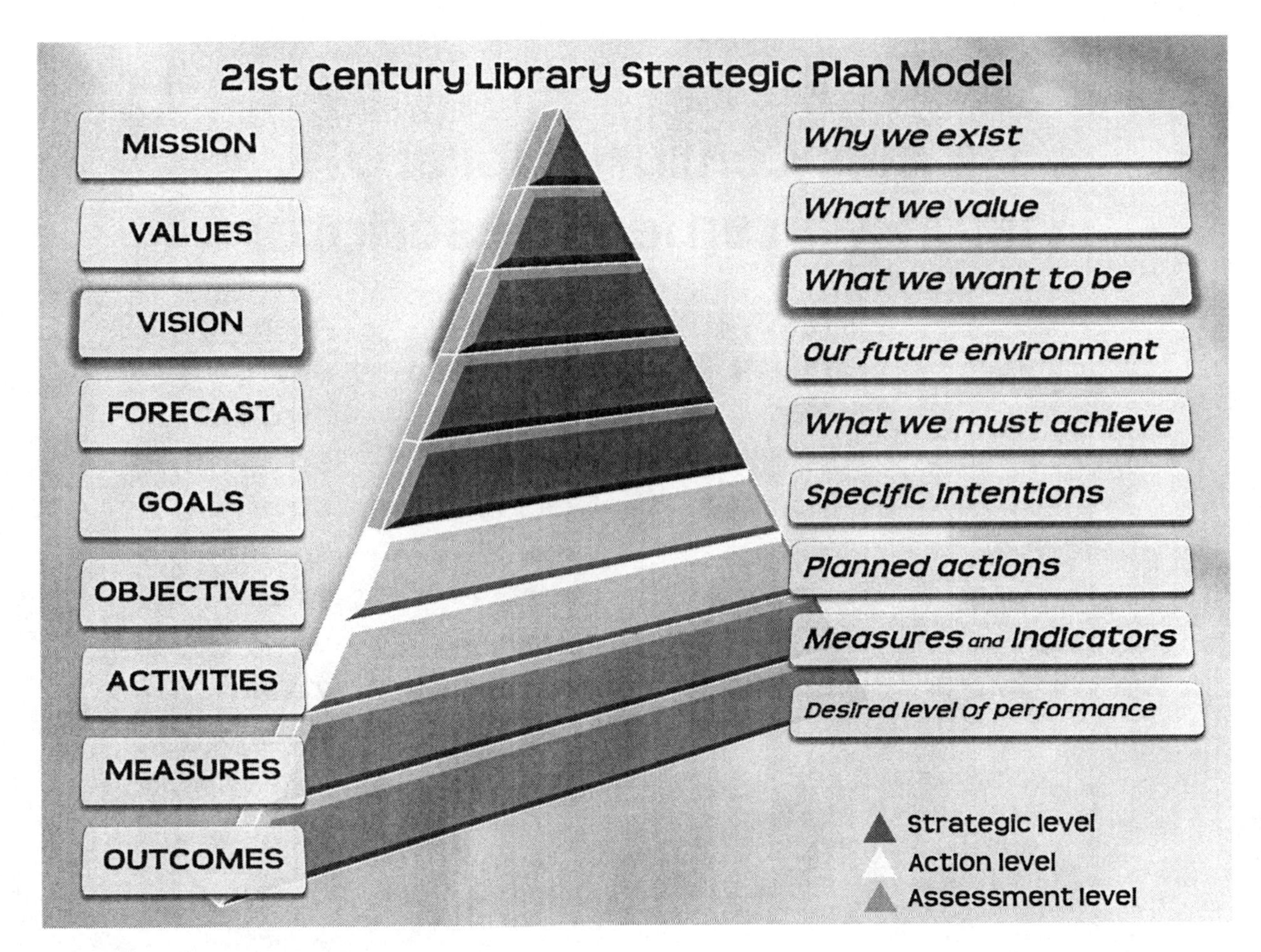

Figure 5.2 Strategic Plan Model—Vision

Vision Statement Template

Since the vision statement is so visionary, it is difficult to offer one template for a vision statement, but it could include the following:

- Library name
- Desire to be . . .
- Vision of . . .
- Other elements that seem appropriate

Again, vision statements do not have to be your own original brainchild of divine inspiration, blood, sweat, and tears. If it doesn't come as a natural creative process, don't torture yourself trying to reinvent the wheel. Borrow, borrow, and borrow.

Vision Descriptors

The descriptor words in Figure 5.3 should be very helpful in creating a vivid description of your library's vision. These are just a few examples.

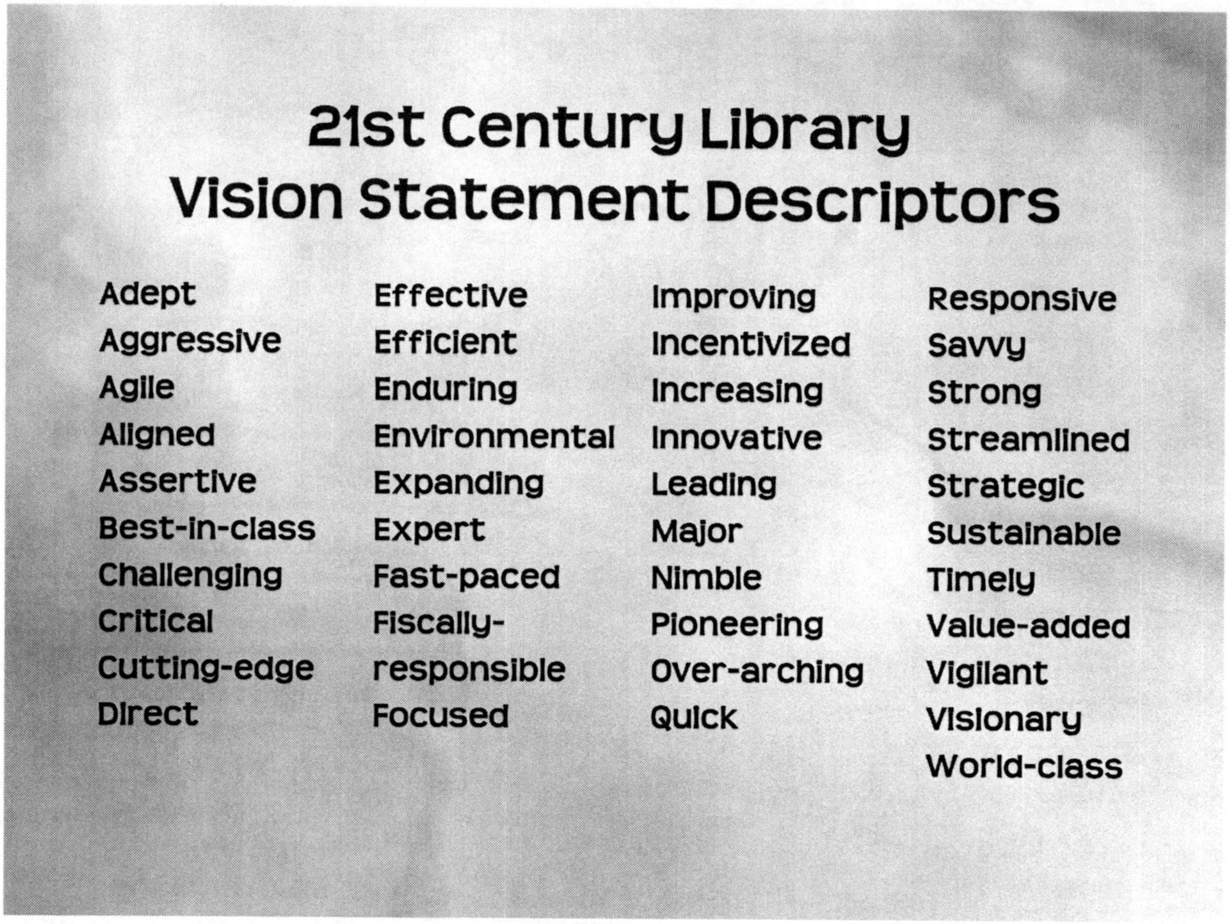

21st Century Library
Vision Statement Descriptors

Adept	Effective	Improving	Responsive
Aggressive	Efficient	Incentivized	Savvy
Agile	Enduring	Increasing	Strong
Aligned	Environmental	Innovative	Streamlined
Assertive	Expanding	Leading	Strategic
Best-in-class	Expert	Major	Sustainable
Challenging	Fast-paced	Nimble	Timely
Critical	Fiscally-	Pioneering	Value-added
Cutting-edge	responsible	Over-arching	Vigilant
Direct	Focused	Quick	Visionary
			World-class

Figure 5.3 Vision Statement Descriptors

PRACTICE

At this point in the planning process you will want to push your people to really dream. The vision statement you create to inspire your organization into the future should come from a place of hope, passion, and idealism. To create something this lofty, you will want to create an environment that fosters those feelings. Arrange meetings and planning sessions that are fun, inspiring, and openly passionate about your library and the profession. Here are a few ideas to facilitate the planning process.

- Start your meeting with participants sharing inspiring stories, such as what the library meant to them as a child, a time when they helped a patron in a deeply meaningful way, what inspired them to choose a career in libraries, and so forth.
- Infuse your meeting with inspirational quotes about the power and importance of library work. One favorite is usually attributed to Andrew Carnegie, "There is not such a cradle of democracy upon the Earth as the Free Public Library."
- Have some fun and lighten the mood or add power and passion by showing clips from movies like the 1999 movie *The Mummy* (remember when the female lead proudly proclaimed I AM A LIBRARIAN!), and the 1957 classic movie *Desk Set* with Spencer Tracy and Katherine Hepburn.
- Use a PowerPoint presentation with inspirational messages including quotes, your organization's history in photos, or interesting pictures that inspire thought and passion about libraries and the future.

Along with creating an environment that is inspiring, you will want to continue to lead the conversation of your group toward visionary, rather than becoming bogged down in the everyday details. While the vision statement must be realistic enough to be usable, reminding participants about the reality of reduced budgets, limited resources, time constraints for projects, current work load, the mission, among others, is probably unnecessary as those issues are ever present in everyone's mind. Not to mention that it tends to dampen the **vision** aspect of the process.

This is the stage of the process where you need to make every effort to guide your group to loftier thoughts in order to create a truly inspiring vision. In reality, the mission will have its time and place as the process proceeds.

This is also the point in the process at which you will begin to recognize the characteristics of your organizational culture. Do people feel free to open up and share their dreams and visionary thoughts about their workplace, or not? How do people react and agree to and improve each other's ideas and visions? Is there a synergy developing within the group that can stimulate the creation of a vision statement that others will be able to support? Who is engaged and who is not? Are you seeing the kind of culture you thought your organization had, or not?

The Question

One simple but profound question will help you determine whether you need to halt the strategic planning process and resolve issues, reassess the values that you just completed, and deal with the organizational change before you continue on with a useful common vision. Every person needs to answer the question individually. You cannot rely on an open conversation where some people are naturally more influential than others to sway individual opinions. Have each person write down their answers anonymously and place them in a bowl to be read individually.

What is your vision for this library that would make you eager to come to work every day? That question makes the workplace **very** personal for every employee. It also identifies what people really think and to what lofty place they aspire. It provides an opportunity to assess whether there are a majority that think alike, and whether there are personality issues that need to be dealt with before proceeding. It is a risky venture, so make the decision to go there **only** if you truly want to know what your people think about your library organization.

EXAMPLE

Sample Vision Statement

"The Xxxxxx Library offers individual enlightenment in every aspect of information and technology in an environment that provides challenge, collaboration, entertainment, and welcome for all through proactive service that meets every need to enhance the quality of life of our customers."

Assessment

Possibly it is a bit too vague and potentially difficult to develop goals and measures, but the intent is to give an example of what your library's vision statement might include.

DERAILMENT

While this is normally considered the most creative part of the entire planning process, it can also be the most frustrating. Each individual's vision of what their library could become will vary widely, which means there will be considerable difference of opinion about which **vision** the library should adopt. People tend to become frustrated and give up if their vision is not adopted, and can remove themselves mentally and emotionally from any further involvement in the planning process.

The director's job is to gain the general consensus talked about earlier in the process to avoid this derailment point. Realistically, not everyone's ideas will be adopted for the plan. This is where any leader must know their people well enough to know how an individual can contribute to the process at some later point. Knowing your people and knowing the process will help ensure that everyone is included at some point along the way.

The majority of people are unlikely to voluntarily sign on for more work so they may limit their vision so as not to have to stretch and perform thereby limiting the amount of additional work or change. No leader can allow this.

SMALL LIBRARY IDEAS

As with the values and guiding principles, the vision for a small library is no different from that of any library of any size. Why? Because **your** vision is whatever you want it to be. It is not dependent on size. Whether you decide to conduct all of the various exercises and actions recommended in this step depends on your assessment of your library and your staff and any others participating in the process.

If your organization is small, one tends to assume that you as director know each individual, the people, and the working environment well. If you believe you know what people think and feel about their library, you may decide to expedite this step in the process. The best practice in this planning model is almost always to do the work, because it will create new ideas and reveal new issues.

CHAPTER 6

Forecast

THEORY

In this strategic plan model, **forecast** is the next step after the mission, values, and vision statements. It comes before the goals and objectives because this step is especially significant in the 21st Century environment due to the rapid changes and highly uncertain future that influence society and all libraries.

Simply put, forecast uses the facts of the present to determine what is most likely to occur in the future. For example: If the property values in your community are the basis for taxation, and these values have experienced a decline in recent years with no appearance of rebound, it is likely that your budget has or will be reduced based upon tax shortfalls and reductions. While this may seem a rather uninspired revelation, it is, in fact, an example of forecasting however obvious. The mission and vision statements outline and describe why the library exists and what it wants to be, but real-world factors in adequate detail must be introduced into the strategic plan for it to be realistic and achievable.

Understanding your library's internal strengths and weaknesses, as well as the external factors you face, will help guide the development of goals and objectives that both capitalize on the strengths and opportunities, as well as improve the weaknesses and address the threats. Self-awareness and a realistic understanding of factors that influence the library's operation will contribute invaluably to goals and objectives that describe the future end-state, desired outcomes that support mission and vision, and direct actions and choices.

Forecasting the Perfect Storm

Remember "The Perfect Storm" phrase that became popular a few years ago? It was used to describe a convergence of environmental conditions that would cause maximum destruction of whatever nature. It was popularized after the 1997 book by the same name by Sebastian Junger, which described unique weather conditions that combined to create a deadly Nor'easter in October 1991, whose damage totaled $208 million with a confirmed death toll of 12 (Junger, 1997). Now whenever conditions appear similarly disastrous for something, it is referred to as a "perfect storm."

When the national economy began to slide into recession, it was referred to as a perfect storm of the housing market collapse, the deficit spending by the government, and massive corporate layoffs (Gross, 2005). News media were reporting a perfect storm of voter distrust in government (Drake, 2010). Business investors were declaring a perfect storm in conditions that stifled real-estate investing (Samples, 2005). Just as we begin to feel more comfortable dealing with this uncertain future, along comes the idea that the future is not uncertain; it's ambiguous (Safian, 2012). Safian asserted that in business (of which libraries are a part) the next 10 to 20 years would be more defined by its changes than by any one model. He claimed that the only pattern was the lack of any pattern; it would be more a time of chaos where everything is situational, and what will work is what people figure out that works. The future is ambiguous.

Recognizing that there is nothing dependable about the future places even greater importance on our efforts to capture a realistic forecast, both internally and externally. Regardless, the strategic plan is your organization's best roadmap to that future for the next few years. As with any journey, having an efficient and successful trip requires knowing where the road blocks and new construction exist, and making the best possible use of all your resources (Figure 6.1).

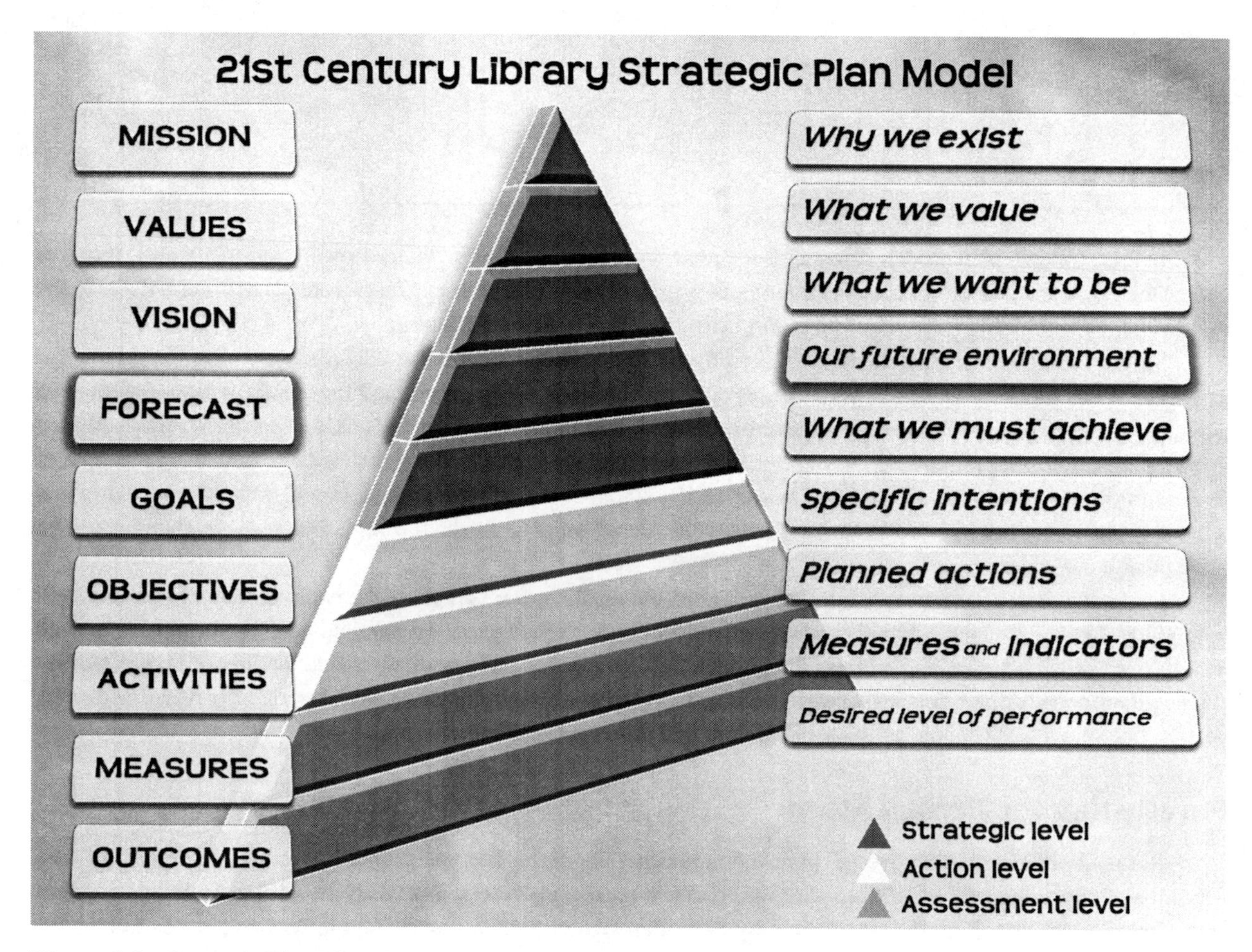

Figure 6.1 Strategic Plan Model—Forecast

Forecasting Using Environmental Scan

In a world that moves and changes so rapidly, pinning down a vision of the future seems a daunting, if not impossible, task. In a profession often driven by constantly changing factors such as technology, finance, media formats, and political climates, it is difficult to imagine what trends will present themselves tomorrow. So then, where to begin?

While there are a number of options for conducting a forecast of the library's future environment, one approach broadly referred to as an environmental scan is a relatively straightforward method of analyzing the internal and external factors that will work to create the future environment in which the organization will most likely exist. As with the environment, business and sociology are frequently changing the terms and methodologies for conducting essentially the same type of research or review.

While the two approaches recommended here are not the most currently popular within business circles, they are still valid, straightforward, easy to understand for everyone participating in the planning process, and can easily be communicated in terms of what results are needed. To accomplish your environmental scan, the following two exercises are recommended.

(1) **S**ocial, **T**echnological, **E**conomic, and **P**olitical (STEP) analysis: This exercise will examine the external factors influencing your organization's future (Wikipedia, 2012).
(2) **S**trengths, **W**eaknesses, **O**pportunities and **T**hreats (SWOT) analysis: This exercise will take a closer look at your organization from an internal and external perspective (Chermack & Kasshanna, 2007).

STEP Analysis

A STEP analysis describes the external environmental factors as they exist in four specific areas. It seeks to identify and assess the external drivers of change that will have an influence on the library and the environment in which it operates in the future. See Figure 6.2. *(More current usage has transposed the factors to spell PEST, but STEP is much more appealing, so the authors have chosen to remain with the earlier variation. Not to mention that searching for resources for "PEST Analysis" will yield more bug than business resources.)*

Social Factors

Social factors include the demographic and cultural aspects of the external environment. These factors affect customer needs and the size of potential markets. Some social factors include the following:

- Changing rural–urban demographics
- Population growth rate
- Local technology adoption
- Attitudes toward libraries
- Interest in supporting local libraries
- Strategic partnerships

Technological Factors

Technological factors can lower barriers to customer interest, increase production levels, and even influence outsourcing decisions. Some technological factors include the following:

- Rate of technological change
- State of technology adoption
- Automation level
- Technology incentives *(e.g., Gates Foundation grants)*

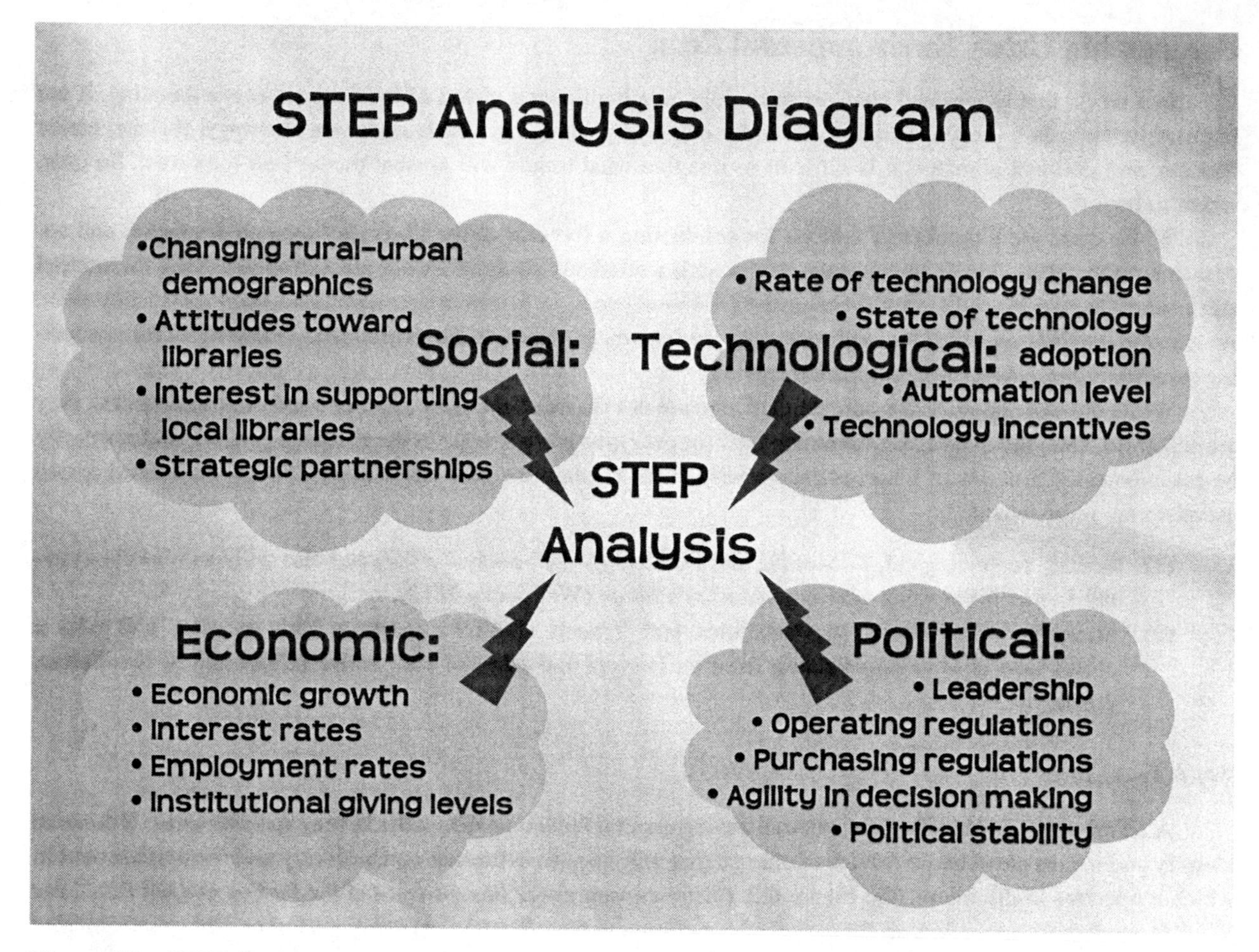

Figure 6.2 STEP Analysis Diagram

Economic Factors

Economic factors affect the purchasing power of potential customers and the organization's cost of capital, which in the case of the library is its ability to obtain funds from its funding authority and outside sources. The following are examples of factors in the economy:

- Economic growth
- Interest rates
- Employment rates
- Institutional giving levels

Political Factors

Political factors include government regulations and legal issues and define both formal and informal rules under which the organization must operate. Some examples include the following:

- Leadership
- Operating regulations
- Purchasing regulations
- Agility in decision making
- Political stability

SWOT Analysis

The SWOT analysis is an exercise that will provide a closer look at your organization. The SWOT analysis provides information that is helpful in matching the organization's resources and capabilities to the competitive environment in which it operates. As such, it is instrumental in strategy formulation and selection.

Environmental factors internal to the organization usually can be classified as strengths or weaknesses. Those factors external to the organization can be classified as opportunities or threats (Figure 6.3).

Strengths

Strengths are those things that you do well. Strengths can be tangible, like loyal customers, efficient distribution channels, very high-quality products, excellent financial condition, cost advantages from being a private entity, and strong brand name. Strengths can also be intangible, like good leadership, strategic insights, customer intelligence (as in detailed knowledge of your patrons), good reputation among customers, and highly skilled workforce.

Weaknesses

Weaknesses are those things that prevent you from doing what you really need to do. Since weaknesses are internal, they are within your control, and often include poor leadership, unskilled workforce, insufficient resources, poor product quality, slow distribution and delivery channels, outdated technologies, lack of planning, a weak brand name, and poor reputation among customers.

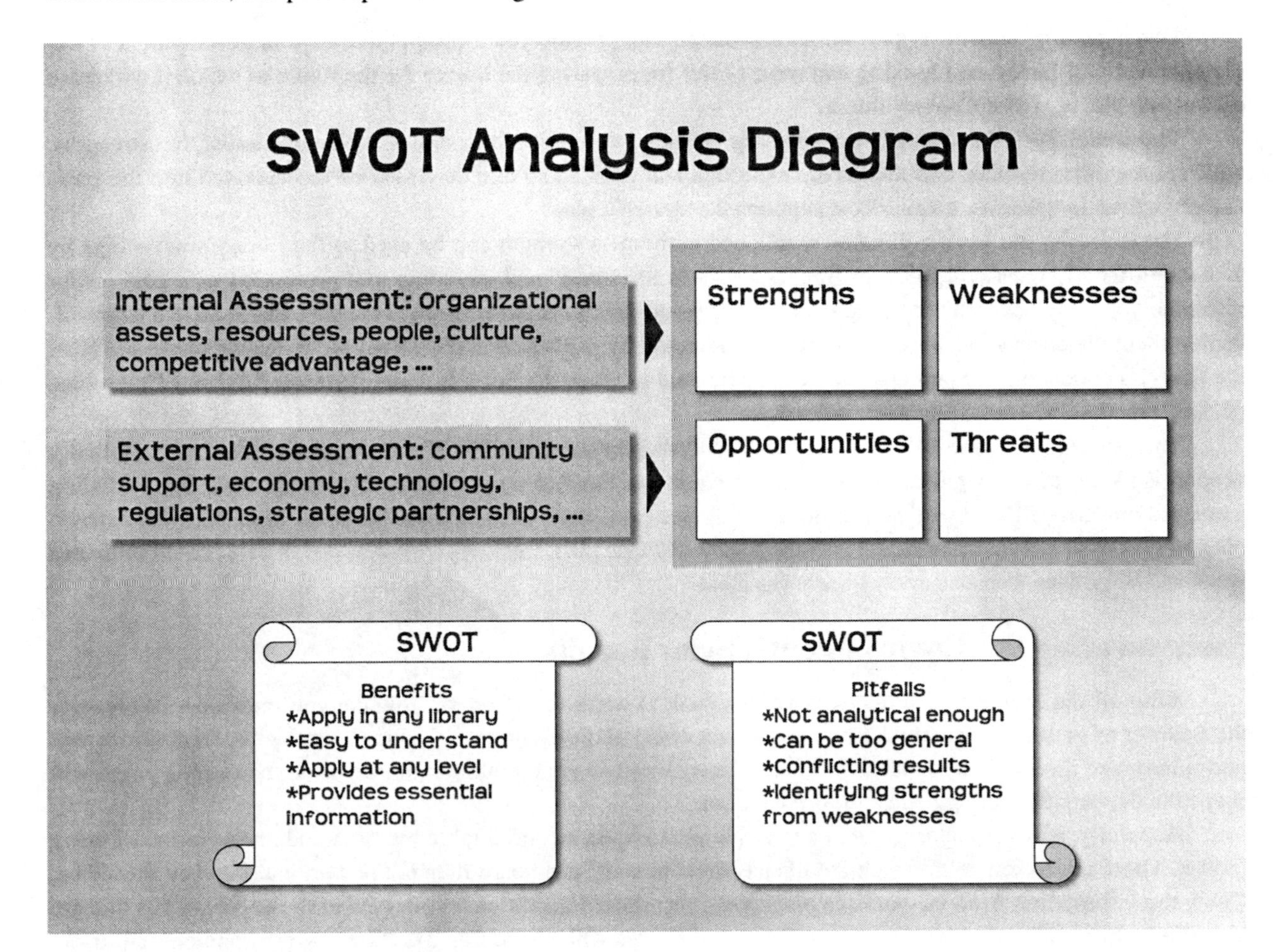

Figure 6.3 SWOT Analysis Diagram

In some cases, a weakness may be the lack of a needed strength. Take a case in which a library has a very large collection. While this collection may be considered a strength because competitors do not have these resources, it also may be considered a weakness if the large collection is poorly organized or labeled, and prevents the customer from easily finding the material they seek.

Opportunities

Opportunities are potential areas for growth and higher performance. Opportunities are external in nature, like untapped segments in the marketplace, dissatisfied customers of your competitors, better economic conditions, more open lending policies, or broader strategic partnerships. Internal opportunities should be classified as strengths, and timing may also be important for capitalizing on opportunities, such as unfulfilled customer needs and adoption of new technologies.

Threats

Threats are challenges confronting the library. External in nature, threats can take a wide range from bad press coverage, shifts in consumer behavior and tastes, emergence of competing products, lack of community support, or new regulations. It may be useful to classify or assign probabilities to threats. The more accurate you are in identifying threats, the better position you are in for dealing with the suddenness of change.

Incorporating SWOT Results

Understanding realistic opportunities and threats can provide you a competitive edge in developing a strategic plan that will be forward looking and more useful for preparing the library for the future in which it will serve customers, that is, a 21st Century future.

The actual SWOT analysis is not normally included as a part of the strategic plan document, but strengths, weaknesses, opportunities, and threats are identified and detailed so that they may be incorporated into the goals and objectives in whatever manner best supports the strategic plan.

For example, the large collection mentioned earlieras a strength can be used to the library's advantage by promoting the "Largest collection of free materials in the state!" and including that promotion as a goal and/or objective, probably under the "community relations" section of your strategic plan. On the other hand, the large collection mentioned earlier as a weakness can be addressed by goals and/or objectives to "Better organize and label the library's collection," or perhaps a more specific goal to adopt the Book Industry Systems Advisory Committee (BISAC) method of organizing your collection.

The same applies to results of the external analysis portion of the SWOT. For example, if lack of community support is identified as a significant threat *(say to continued funding support, or even a bond issue)*, then including goals and objectives that overcome that threat *(such as an energetic advocacy campaign, or more beneficial strategic partnerships)* make a more useful and productive strategic plan. Both opportunities and threats should influence goals and objectives, because *every* library has them.

Incorporating the Environmental Scan Results

After all the exercises and analyses are finished, to make the effort worthwhile you must now incorporate the findings of your environmental scan into the rest of the planning process. Using the strengths, weaknesses, opportunities, and threats that you have outlined as you formulate your goals and objectives in the coming pages will shape the development of realistic and focused ones.

Hopefully, it is very apparent that a strategic plan requires considerable research and investigation of many factors. These are factors with which the library director, staff, and board may not be familiar, but they should be. Given the information from an environmental scan, you should match your strengths to the opportunities that are identified while addressing weaknesses and external threats. Otherwise this 21st Century environment will make your library's survival very difficult.

What they didn't teach you in library school about surviving both as a librarian and as a library in the 21st Century environment is monumental. We must learn new principles and approaches to success for ourselves and share the lessons learned. We must begin to think outside the box, open our eyes to outside influences, adopt practices from business, become familiar with SWOT and STEP factors, and work harder than ever to make the library relevant in the 21st Century. Would you rather be stereotyped as a shusher or respected as an entrepreneur?

PRACTICE

As you read through the theory portion of this chapter, if you never had to go back and reread a particular section of description of SWOT or STEP analysis, then in all likelihood you are already familiar with the concepts. You have either used them in previous planning or studied them in school at some point. For many, the concepts can be a bit confusing and require a bit of practice and explanation to understand how the research works and can be effectively incorporated.

With that in mind, when you are ready to move to the forecast step with your committee or staff you will want to consider how you plan to complete the research steps in the most effective manner possible. In previous steps, it has been recommended that you take the time to explain in full the importance of each step and how it fits into the overall plan. This inclusive openness traditionally garners the most valuable input from your group.

However, as you begin forecasting you may consider altering that approach. Remember in this step you are, in essence, attempting to create an assessment of what the library's future environment will look like. The very nature of that task is daunting to even the most fearless planner. You should find that breaking the process into manageable bites for your group will provide more realistic and accurate results.

Rather than greeting your committee or staff with the starting sentence, "Today we will be doing a SWOT analysis," you might consider saying, "Today we are going to talk about our library's strengths and weaknesses." Begin a brainstorm session in this fashion and see where the conversation goes. Then move to "What opportunities and threats to our organization, services, and profession do you believe exist?" Have a member of your group write the responses on a white board. Use a separate board or area of board for each of the four categories of strength, weakness, opportunity, and threat. Once you feel the conversation has garnered all usable responses and has wound down naturally, explain to your group the importance and relationship between the four elements. Ask if anyone observes any patterns or trends in the lists. Document anything your group identifies for later use.

In a second meeting, you can follow up with a review of the previous brainstormed ideas and ask if anyone has had any additional thoughts. As your group discussion moves toward external influences, ask your staff to delve further into the external. As a guide, present them with the four areas of social, technological, economic, and political environments. Exactly as you previously did with the SWOT analysis exercise, you have now moved your group into the STEP analysis with no anxiety or stress. You have moved the conversation organically in a manner that will produce the most authentic responses.

In addition to staff, library trustees or a board of directors can be extremely valuable assets in this process, especially if the appointing authority has chosen a diverse and experienced board that has dealt with such planning processes in other organizations. Most organizations in all sectors deal with strategic planning, and the ability to apply that experience to the library's strategic plan will go far in causing the planning process to produce a highly worthwhile and visionary plan.

DERAILMENT

So much can derail the process in this phase; it is difficult to elaborate on everything. The largest roadblock to a successful forecasting effort is losing your group in the process of the analysis. As the leader, you can guide the group easily to results rather than forcing them to become mired in the details of the exploration. Again, only the group leader truly needs to be fluent in the details of the SWOT and STEP analyses. Allowing the group members to focus on bite-sized pieces of the process rather than presenting them with the task of predicting the future will reduce the pressure of such an arduous task.

Fundamentally, a useful and accurate forecast requires someone who understands the process as well as the elements involved in the forecast, and is able to apply the library's resources to develop answers or, at the very least, educated estimates. If you do not have someone who has some slight familiarity with forecasting, you should consider seeking outside assistance.

As with previous steps it is vital to create an environment that is open and honest. To receive honest answers concerning issues such as organizational weaknesses, staff members must feel confident that they can speak freely without fear of reprisals or judgment. Also, as you discuss larger philosophical issues such as environmental threats and spit-balling over the next big technological trend, you must create a spirit of open sharing where all staff members regardless of position, education, or experience will feel comfortable sharing ideas.

For example, the first staffer to bring up the idea of the latest trend in social media may not be a more experienced librarian. Instead, it may be your high-school-age page that has a finger on the pulse of the next generation and what this age group is looking for in information technology and sharing. If that page does not feel safe from ridicule or scorn when sharing a completely new and untested idea, it is most likely that you will never have the opportunity to hear from them.

Finally, one of the most important factors for the success of leaders and managers who have "been there, done that" is to be open. Whether an idea is new or old, let it roll out and breathe for a while. It is easy after a certain point in a long career to quickly dismiss an idea with "oh, we tried that years ago . . ." or some other equally condescending dismissal. Fight the urge to do that. Remember when everything was fresh and new and the world was awash with limitless possibilities. Allow your staff the same luxury to dream big, work big, and succeed big. Is the possibility there to fail big? Of course, it always will be. But remember what your heart and mind may have said a decade or two ago when you were in the other chair "just because it did not work then does not mean it will not work now." Try!

What of those audaciously new ideas? Remember the old adage, "New ideas are usually suspect for no reason other than that they are new." Let the ideas soar! If you have done your job and hired good people and trained them well, allow them to soar.

SMALL LIBRARY IDEAS

As stated earlier, in most cases, the small library has limited resources and expertise to pursue a detailed and in-depth strategic planning process. Regarding the forecast, this is especially true. It is unlikely that most library staff in a small town will have a business background to be familiar with this type of forecast. However, it is entirely likely that there are capable business people, educators, community leaders, or others within the community who do have the necessary expertise and would be willing to help their library.

If you are in a small library and have followed the advice of previous chapters then you likely have a planning committee comprised of some of these very people. Tap into them and find the person you feel has the most experience with forecasting and ask them for assistance. If you find yourself at this step without anyone in your group with the necessary expertise, recruit someone, even if you have to hire them. It will be money well spent. The more stakeholders and community leaders you incorporate into your plan, the more support you will have as you implement and move forward.

CHAPTER 7

Goals and Objectives

THEORY

A visionary strategic plan is monumentally important to becoming a good library, but it is **critical** to providing a library that is highly relevant to a 21st Century community. Becoming a highly relevant library in the future environment of your community is venturing into totally unknown territory because there are so many unknown and unfamiliar factors and influences involved as stated throughout this book. Since these factors and influences are changing so rapidly, attempting to accomplish the necessary **goals and objectives** of a 21st Century Library without a strategic plan is unimaginable. Where would you begin? What activities would you select to receive those critically limited resources, or would you just allow staff to randomly do their own thing? How will you know when you've achieved any goals or objectives leading toward your mission?

Some librarians think planning strategically or otherwise is a tired old library standard with which everybody is familiar but really can just be ignored. Unfortunately, it's not something to be ignored when it comes to a strategic plan to guide your public library into this uncertain 21st Century environment. There is too much at stake, including the survival of your library, to simply keep pursuing business as usual and hope for the best.

What's the Difference?

This is usually the big question when it comes to developing goals and objectives based on the obvious question—"Why is it always goals *and* objectives?" Actually, some use the terms goals and objectives interchangeably and synonymously, and you will find in a search of literature that often they are combined or even transposed. In the context of this 21st Century Library Strategic Plan Model, the distinction between goals and objectives is important and practical.

To begin with, goals come before objectives and relate directly to the mission statement, while objectives are created with their only purpose being to achieve goals. Most significant is that a particular goal is important on its own; however, while they are also important, objectives are not important by themselves. Alone, out of the context of goals, objectives could be just a random list of things the library staff wants to do, a list of activities that have always been done. That business as usual list probably does not and will not contribute to achieving a necessary, new, more relevant mission.

You will decide what objectives **must** be accomplished in order to achieve a goal. Some questions to consider are as follows:

- Do you and your staff need training?
- Do you need some resource or resources missing from the library?
- Do you need to establish a beneficial partnership or collaboration that does not exist now?
- Do you need some new technology?
- Are there objectives that are prerequisite to others?

By developing the answers to these and many more questions you will be developing your objectives.

Another key point is that objectives are much more than activities. Objectives are a description of how to accomplish goals, and they still contain some challenge and options for "How To . . .," while activities are more simply things that you just do. If an objective does not work to help achieve its goal, modify, or replace it so that it does. Develop as many objectives as it takes to achieve the goal they support.

Goal versus Objective

Goal	**Objective**
Directly relates to mission statement	Supports achievement of its goal
Briefly stated in a few words	More descriptive, longer statement
General and broad scope	Specific and narrow scope
Covers longer time period (three years)	Covers shorter time period (one year)
More difficult to measure independently	Easily measured
Less tangible	Very tangible

Figure 7.1 represents the place of Goals within the 21st Century Library Strategic Plan Model. They are subordinate to Mission and come after the rest of the strategic level planning is accomplished.

Developing Goals

Goals are the desired results in various areas, expressed in general terms about what we want to achieve to accomplish the mission. They are generally long-term, open-ended, and sometimes never 100 percent achieved, because, as has been stated, the strategic plan is a living document. Goals can change, especially if they are not written well enough during the first iteration to achieve the mission or provide appropriate parameters for the objectives. Working toward our goals takes us toward our mission, using our vision as motivation, and our values as a guide.

<u>Goals should be</u>

- derived from the mission statement;
- formulated to achieve the library's mission and vision;
- written broad in scope but easily understood, clear, and concise;
- appear to be realistic and achievable *based on the library's resources*;
- designed to be measurable and able to be tracked and evaluated *as to whether they have been achieved*; and
- created to be meaningful *because goals make or break the library's mission*.

Along with goals striving to achieve the library's vision and mission, they must also be aligned to the library's values. Goals should be seen as opportunities for the library staff to accomplish, not a burden that is out of reach or

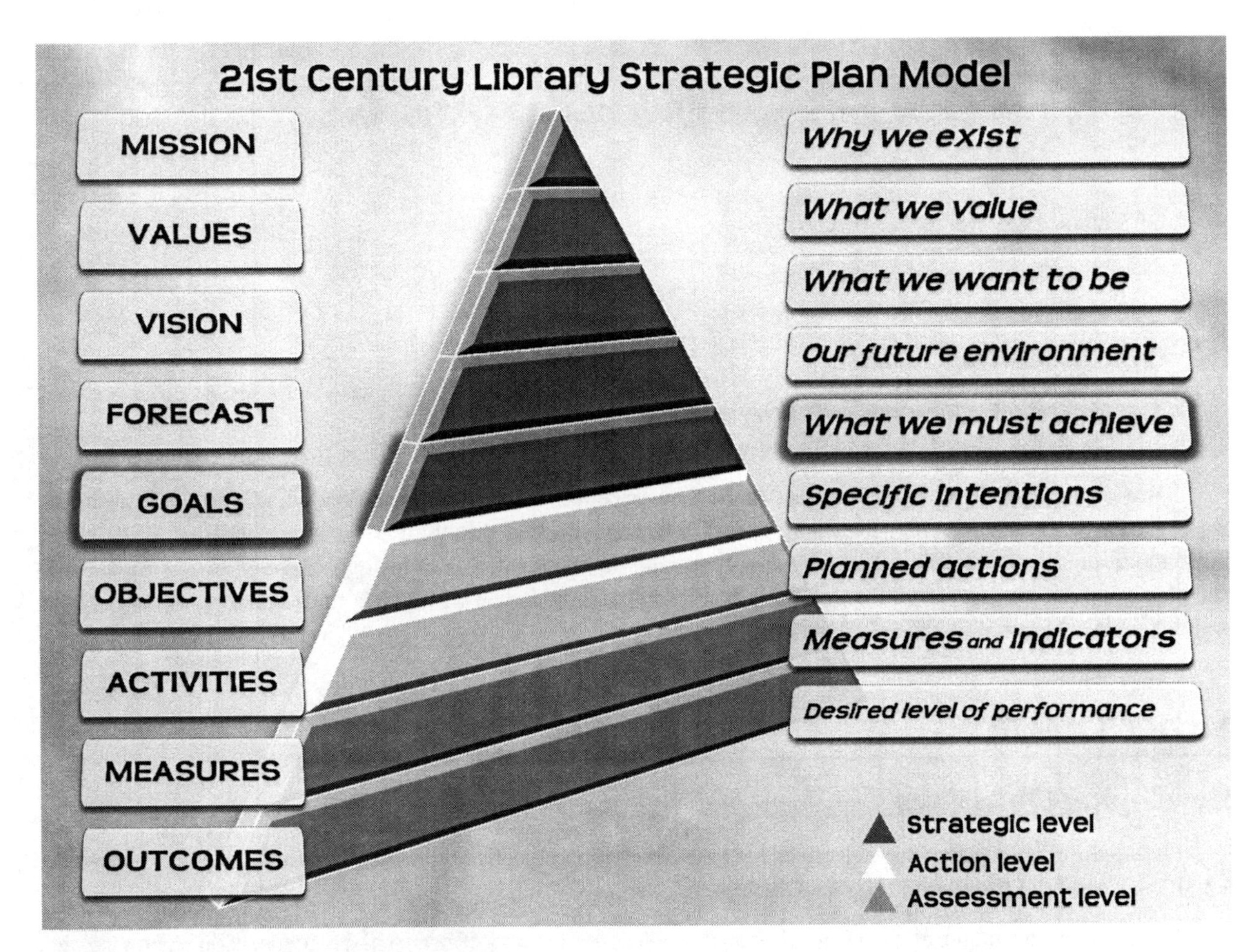

Figure 7.1 Strategic Plan Model—Goals

a fanciful wish list. Goals can be established for the entire library and for operational units, for example, technical services, circulation, programing, and so forth.

The most important aspect of developing goals is gaining commitment to achieve them from everyone involved with the library. Good communication during the development process is essential, and once established they should be disseminated widely and discussed openly.

PRACTICE

It can be difficult to keep a firm grasp on the scope and place of goals versus objectives. Feeling clear headed about the differences is vital to the leader of the planning process, as well as to the participants. Often it is easier to keep a clear picture in your mind if you apply the theory to something a bit more familiar.

Almost everyone has made a few New Year's resolutions at some point in their life. Resolutions such as losing weight, learning a language, saving money, living greener, getting a better job, and others often top the list. Unfortunately, as many can attest, the success rate of New Year's resolutions is fairly poor. Why is that? Are they unrealistic? Thousands of people every year lose weight, learn languages, save money, go green, or get new jobs. The failure rate of these resolutions cannot be that they are hopelessly unrealistic. Instead, it is much more likely that they simply are not implemented in the first place or are approached with a lack of any real commitment or strategy.

Imagine if, in place of a New Year's resolution, you created a New Year's strategic plan. In considering this, it will allow a firmer grasp of the difference between goals and objectives. If you were to take one of the most popular resolutions of losing weight and apply it to goals and objectives, how would that look?

Goal: Be healthy

Objective: Lose weight

> **Activity:** Stop eating after 7 P.M.
> **Activity:** Eat smaller serving portions

Objective: Exercise

> **Activity:** Go for a long walk every weekend
> **Activity:** Ride the bike to the store

You can see that the goal, as discussed in the theory section, is long-term, open-ended, and broad. In contrast, the objective is clearly specific, measurable, and, when approached through the activities outlined, achievable. From this example, it should be clear why simply tossing out the resolution of losing weight without a framework and plan often dooms that resolution to failure. It should also provide you with a clear understanding of the purpose and differences between goals and objectives.

MORE THEORY

Developing Objectives

It is helpful here to explore objectives because developing objectives specifically to achieve goals and guide activities is essential for several reasons. Objectives:

- provide the target at which to aim *so* that all activities and efforts will be focused on achieving the objective;
- give staff direction as to what they will be achieving;
- provide a clearly defined guide to reaching the goal;
- provide the means to evaluate the progress of achieving a goal;
- contribute to achieving the goal;
- focus on the outcomes; and
- offer a guide to measure success.

Developing Objectives is the beginning step for the action level of the 21st Century Strategic Plan Model, and begins the level at which all library staff must be involved in the planning process. The process of developing objectives could include listing a dozen or more possible objectives that come to mind for a specific goal, and then scrutinizing each to decide whether it will contribute to achieving that goal and whether it is realistic, achievable, and measurable (Figure 7.2). Just because an objective sounds like a great idea, doesn't mean it is the right objective for your library at the present time. Objectives must meet certain criteria to be worthwhile and useful. Possibly the best method for developing and selecting objectives is the **S**pecific, **M**easurable, **A**chievable, **R**elevant, and **T**ime-bound (SMART) approach (Meyer, 2003).

Specific

When it comes to strategic planning, specific means something that is easily identified and understood, and meets the criteria outlined earlier. Individual objectives should not encompass more than one aspect of a goal, but be specific in addressing each of the elements that reasonably comprise the goal, regardless of how many or how

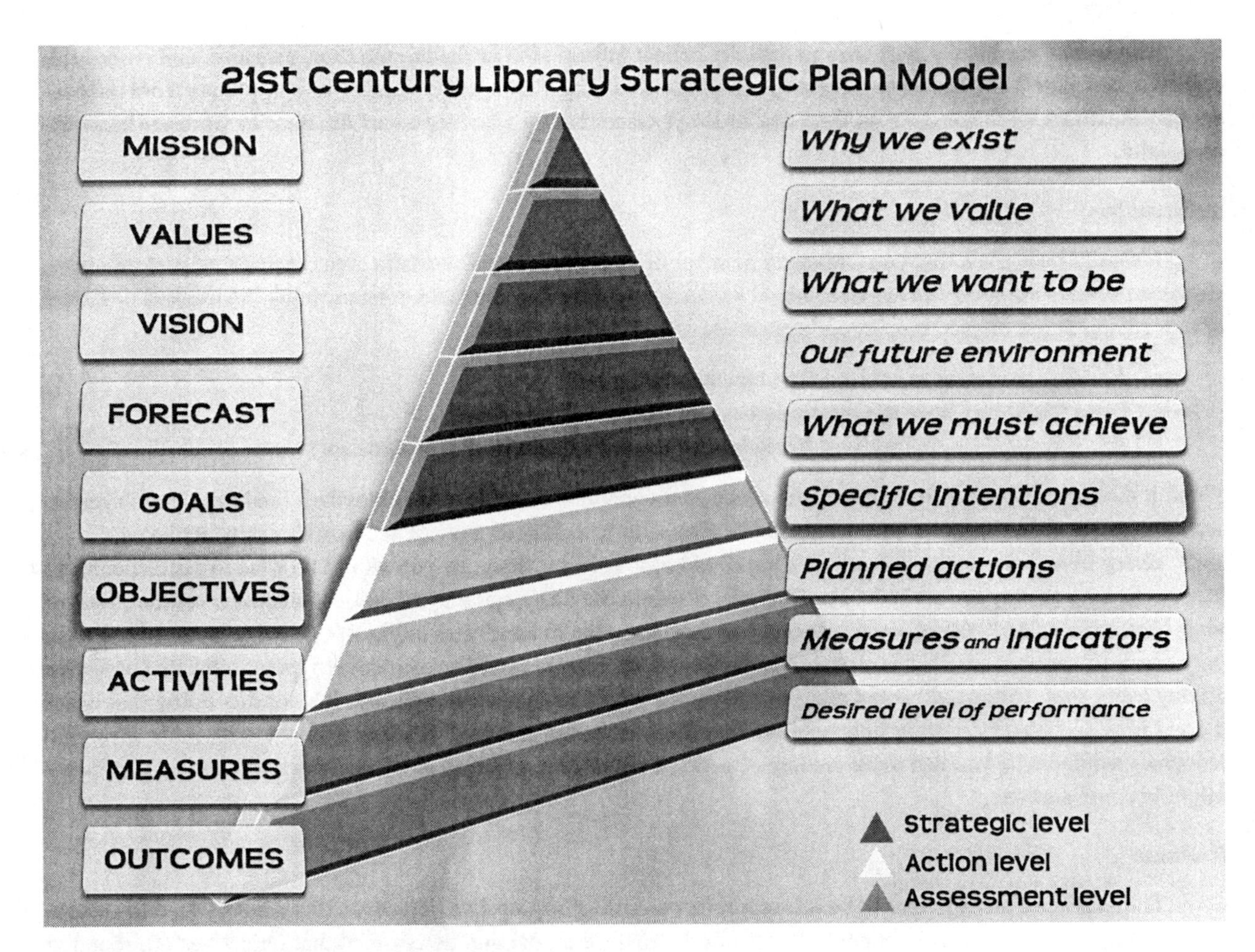

Figure 7.2 Strategic Plan Model—Objectives

few objectives are chosen. Too few end up being a mirror of the goal without being useful in developing activities. Too many may be actually describing the activities of the plan rather than really being objectives.

For example, if you tell someone, "I need this report in several copies," you did not provide them with a specific instruction. It is unclear what "several" means. It also does not communicate a time frame for the action. A much better instruction would be: "I need this report in 5 copies, collated and stapled, before close of business today." In similar manner, a well-crafted objective will communicate exactly what you expect and will have less chances to fail in delivering the desired result.

Measurable

When an objective is measurable, that implies the necessity that it has the capability to be measured, to track the activities associated with the objective, and to know when it has been achieved. Every committee or staff must have in place a system of clear procedures of how objectives and activities will be monitored, measured, and recorded. If an objective and the activities pertaining to it cannot be quantified, it is most likely that the objective is poorly developed and should be reconsidered.

For example, "Improve customer service" is a general goal, and without more specific details of objectives and activities is not easily measured. However, the objective to "Ensure the library is ready to serve the customers at opening time every day" is more easily measured, a major distinction between goals and objectives. By adding activities under objectives, for example, "Open the doors to the library on time every day," measurability becomes more possible. Were the doors open on time or not, or how many days were they delayed and why?

The means the library staff uses to actually collect information or data to monitor, measure, and record this objective can vary from formal to informal, complicated to easy. Perhaps, the number of complaints from customers that the doors were not open on time can be simply recorded by whoever opens the door or whoever hears the complaint.

Achievable

It should be a given that you and every member of your library staff wants to give outstanding performances. However, when setting objectives, one should seriously consider first the factors determining the success or failure of objectives. Think of your employees' capacities and of their motivation.

- Are they sufficient to achieve the objectives being set?
- Does the library have the means and capabilities to achieve them?
- Are your goals and objectives likely headed toward success or disappointment?

Think it through and be honest and realistic about your capability to achieve the objectives (and even goals) you've set. Always set objectives that have a reasonable chance to be achieved, but not necessarily easily achieved.

Every library must stretch itself if it hopes to improve in anything, so you would be wise to set difficult objectives as long as they are realistic. For example, if within the library goal of "Excellent customer service," one of your objectives was to "Greet every customer as they enter the library," that might not be achievable. If you have only one staff member working circulation at the front desk, no one would be available to accomplish that objective all day every day. This would mean that your objective would not get accomplished. It's not that doing that is not a good idea and could certainly help achieve "excellent customer service." It's that it is not achievable given the resources available. If you had more resources, perhaps volunteers, greeting every customer who enters the library might become realistic.

Relevant

The quality of an objective to be relevant refers to setting appropriate objectives that actually lead to achieving the goal they support. It is important to seriously analyze a goal and determine what objectives are required to achieve it, and then select from the various alternatives of how to achieve those objectives that are relevant and achievable. Rather than having an objective of greeting every customer who comes through the door, a relevant objective might be for every staff member to greet each customer they encounter, wherever they encounter them in the library. In that way, it is a natural situation, not contrived, and it accomplishes the same goal of excellent customer service, and certainly is relevant.

Time-bound

This aspect is simply establishing a realistic and appropriate time frame for achieving an objective. Many objectives lend themselves to a specific time frame of when it should start and when it should be achieved. Having a time frame specified makes it easier to measure and determine if it has been achieved. Some activities that support objectives are daily, others are weekly or longer, and these objectives simply need to be identified so the measurement can be appropriate, perhaps annually. Where the activities are not routine, that is, they are only performed as needed, the time frame is even more important so that when it comes to allocation of resources, the objective can be more easily funded or provided for by appropriate resources.

MORE PRACTICE

In previous "Practice" sections of this book, it has been emphasized that the process leader should guide and assist but not force ideas into the planning process. As you approach the creation of goals and objectives, you will often find yourself cutting closer to that line to help guide your group in differentiating which elements are goals and which are objectives. Also, and more important, you will be required to advise them on the creation of a goal to contain a worthy objective. While in theory the objectives will organically grow from the goals, in reality ideas that fall into both levels of the plan will be generated during the planning process. Your responsibility as the leader and guide of the process is to ensure that each worthy idea finds a home.

You may find during brainstorming with your group that a pattern of objectives are emerging that have not been addressed by a goal. You will need to bring that to the group's attention. In all likelihood they will then look to create a goal that will wrap the objectives in a nice package that fits neatly into the plan. On the converse, if you find a single objective still "homeless" at the end of your planning, the group may decide that, while worthy, it does not fill a need or goal in the plan that is of significant enough importance for inclusion.

An example of being measurable is the following. "Improve customer service" is a fairly general goal. Without more specific details of the objectives and activities it would be almost impossible to measure. However, the objective to "Ensure the library is ready to serve the customers at opening time every day" is more easily measured. By adding activities under objectives, like, "Open the doors to the library on time every day," measurability becomes more cut and dried. Were the doors open on time, or not?

An example of developing an achievable objective was the one within the library goal of "Excellent customer service," where one of your objectives was to "Greet every customer as they enter the library." That might not be achievable unless you have the personnel resources to actually accomplish it, no matter how desirable it is.

STILL MORE THEORY

Incorporating Opportunity

You may be asking yourself, "What about flexibility to seize opportunities that arise 'out of the blue'?" How do those fit into this strategic plan process? Very easily. If you think about what kind of opportunity might crop up that you and your library would be interested in taking advantage of and participating in, it would most likely be one that fits with your mission, goals, objectives, and activities. It will most likely be closely related to something you already do, or at least something that fits with what your library is and what you and your staff do. In which case, you should easily be able to include that into your next revision of your strategic plan in its appropriate place under an existing goal as an objective with activities. You may want to create a new goal with new objectives specific to this new opportunity. Whatever works for your situation is easily doable.

What if something out of the blue looks like an awesome opportunity, but you can't find a fit within your existing mission, goals or objectives? It happens. It could be something that changes the way you do business, or something that alters or creates a new position, or drastically changes the library in some profound way. This could be an awesome challenge! Don't hesitate to do it, and if it is truly successful and sustainable, you can simply deal with it during your next revision of the strategic plan. Incorporate it where it will fit, either as part of the mission, or as a goal. By the time the next review rolls around you should have a good understanding of this new opportunity and how you may have had to adjust your other objectives and activities, as well as resource allocations to incorporate it into your mission.

Planned Abandonment

Similarly as with new opportunities, review of your strategic plan should include abandoning old programs or operations that no longer fit with your mission priorities. One of the things librarians traditionally have trouble with is weeding and discontinuing programs. Realistically, a library staff cannot do everything, and they cannot keep adding programs and services any more than they can keep adding collection without weeding. You must prioritize what your library staff can and should do, and make serious decisions about abandoning those things that are no longer relevant.

STILL MORE PRACTICE

As technology advancements continue in the library field, it seems inevitable that a transition from print to digital collections will happen. Evidence is strong that customers are demanding more digital resources, and therefore, eventually, general print collections will be replaced by digital materials. Having a plan that addresses that transition based on customer needs and available resources is smart planning. Describing this transition goal in objectives and activities is one way to make it happen.

Sample Goals and Objectives for Strategic Partnerships

One of the areas of planning that has developed from a 21st Century environment deals with strategic partnerships. Considering that this is a relatively new area of library endeavor, here is a suggestion about incorporating it into your next strategic plan. Remember that goals are the desired results we want to achieve to accomplish the mission, expressed in general terms.

Goal #7—Develop strategic partnerships.

Expressed in general terms, this Goal is broad enough to allow for more specific Objectives.

Objective #O7.1—Seek out organizations, companies, agencies of any type within the community that have potential strategic partnership value to the library.

This description defines a specific objective to be proactive in determining what entities within your community have potential benefits for the library through a strategic partnership.

Activity #A7.1.1—Conduct preliminary research to better understand which organizations, companies, or agencies have potential benefits as strategic partners.

Activity #A7.1.2—Conduct preliminary research to better understand what the identified potential strategic partners do.

Activity #A7.1.3—Conduct more in-depth research to better understand what the potential strategic partners' library service needs may be.

Activity #A7.1.4—Prioritize community entities on the basis of the most potentially beneficial partnership for Xxxxx Library.

Objective #O7.2—Contact organizations, companies, and agencies with potential strategic value within the community that potentially have library service needs that Xxxxx Library can provide.

This description defines a specific objective to be proactive in determining what entities within your community have library service needs that are within your capabilities. This is also part of knowing your community's library service needs.

Activity #A7.2.1—Develop a succinct, appealing, business-like brochure of library services to leave with the people with whom you will meet.

Activity #A7.2.2—Schedule visits with leaders of potential partners to discuss their potential library service needs, highest priority first.

Objective #O7.3—Conclude the details of a strategic partnership with organizations, companies, and agencies that expressed interest in a partnership with Xxxxx Library.

This description defines a specific objective to follow-up on those opportunities that materialize as a result of your strategic partnership efforts.

Activity #A7.3.1—Clarify the details of specific partnerships.

Activity #A7.3.2—Assess resources necessary to fulfill obligations of a partnership.

Activity #A7.3.3—Prepare plans to manage a partnership.

The sample discussed in the preceding pages is what your pre-strategic partnership plan might look like. What about when you actually establish a strategic partnership that impacts your goals, resource allocation, and so forth? How do you revise your strategic plan?

After you have secured and cultivated a strategic partnership for your library, it will change your situation enough to incorporate the existence of that partnership into your strategic plan.

- How are you going to manage the details of this partnership?
- What resources are required to accomplish the requirements of this partnership?
- What are the measures and outcomes related to this partnership?
- How will you know if you are succeeding in your obligations?
- How will you know if this partnership is actually beneficial to the library, and beneficial to your mission?

Here is another suggestion for established partnerships. The objectives change after one has been established.

Objective #O8.1—Provide library services for XYZ Organization in accordance with the partnership memo of understanding (MOU).

Activity #A8.1.1—Revise the library collection development policy to include technical materials relevant to XYZ Organization's library services needs.

Activity #A8.1.2—Conduct training for reference and acquisition staff to become familiar with technical materials relevant to XYZ Organization.

Activity #A8.1.3—Conduct resource allocation review to prioritize acquisition of technical materials related to XYZ Organization partnership.

All of these issues related to a new strategic partnership need to become a part of your library's strategic plan, because when you actually do establish a new strategic partnership goal it brings with it new and necessary objectives, activities, measures, outcomes, and unquestionably resource allocation, all of which impact the overall strategic plan. Don't forget, your strategic plan is a living document.

DERAILMENT

As outlined previously, the easiest way to get derailed during the goals and objectives part of the process is through a lack of understanding of the purposes and distinctions between the two. Getting goals and objectives confused is easy if they are not well understood. This includes understanding how to write each, and using the SMART guidelines. What you may end up with are goals that should be objectives, and vice versa.

Another easy sidetrack is developing goals that do not support the mission, and not developing goals that do support the mission. People obviously need to understand the mission statement and need to accept that it is what will guide the process from here on. If people are still hung up on the mission, haven't accepted it, or still question what it means, they will not be able to develop effective and meaningful goals. Without good goals, there won't be good objectives. If you continue to encounter either resistance or confusion in the creation of goals and objectives that support the mission, you may need to pause and revisit the mission to ensure it still has the buy-in and support necessary for success. Regardless of what it takes to get through the goals and objectives, the group **must** keep progressing, because the risk of burnout increases with every phase. Spending too much time on any one phase only increases that risk of burnout.

The leader must be vigilant at every phase to observe people wanting to revert to the Old Plan. Assuming that it was actually used to guide the organization in the past, it is known and familiar. Even if it was a paperweight or doorstop, people will want to drag it out and refer back to what was acceptable. It's the easy way to get through this strategic planning process. Unfortunately, it won't give you a useful or meaningful plan that will guide the library into the future, let alone help you become a 21st Century Library.

Be cautious about allowing the inclusion of unmet goals from previous plans. Be suspect of the often used phrase, "Well since we did not complete this one it should be included because it is still important," or "We need to keep this in the plan since we are still working on it." The group should look at each attempted inclusion of an old goal or objective and ask, "Why wasn't it completed?", "Is it still meaningful to our new Mission?", and "Are we still headed in that direction?"

One big pitfall comes when the plan is nearing completion and things are not turning out as well as the leadership anticipated. A strong inclination surfaces to revise goals and objectives to make them more in line with what the leadership wants the library staff to achieve. By tweaking the goals and/or objectives, the leaders are essentially creating a new plan that staff may not understand. They won't understand the purpose of the changes or why the changes were made. Leadership will lose all the staff buy-in that was created through the process, and staff will begin to feel like the leadership's interest in change and participation was simply lip service. There is no more demoralizing situation than at the end of the strategic planning process for the plan to be significantly different than what staff members worked on and agreed to.

Leaders must have a sincere commitment to allow the process to result in what the members of the organization want their library to be within reason. Otherwise, it would be better not to even try this strategic planning process. Instead, do it yourself and try to convince staff to adopt it, or just push it through. Whatever works for your library.

It is easy to give up and resort to the half-hearted copying of old goals and objectives, and other items; and very much more difficult to do the work necessary to create a worthwhile and useful plan to help guide your library into the uncertain future, provide the important services to make your library relevant and valuable in a 21st Century community, capitalize on the limited resources available to make that happen, and make every resource, especially human resources, contribute toward that mission.

While some think good librarianship is all that is required to forge into the 21st Century future, in reality those things cannot be accomplished by the seat of anyone's pants. They require significant communication, change, and planning.

SMALL LIBRARY IDEAS

Considerable hard work goes into developing worthwhile goals and objectives for any library. A small library with limited staff and other resources can feel overwhelmed by the prospect of writing goals and objectives that will actually help improve the library's resources and services making it a better institution in the 21st Century. This may be a good place to borrow some ideas from other library organizations. That is not to suggest that you should simply copy goals or objectives from other libraries, but borrow ideas.

Many libraries have strategic plans posted on their websites. Some publish just the mission, vision, and goals on one web page for the public. Others make the entire plan available with a link to a PDF document. Some will provide both. Look for those complete plan documents. Consider what that library staff and committee have developed. Consider whether these goals or objectives will provide you with valuable ideas for your library, at least it will help you get started and make some progress.

Be certain to use the SMART guidelines to ensure that you really do have useful goals and objectives. Just because they read well doesn't mean they will actually help you fulfill your plan requirements. Don't be swayed by an attractive sounding goal or objective and adopt it for your plan. It must pass the same test as if you developed it yourself in order for it to be useable. Some good examples of library goals and objectives are from the institutions listed here contained on their website.

Seattle (WA) Public Library, http://www.spl.org/about-the-library/strategic-planning/goals-and-objectives
Cornell University Library, http://www.library.cornell.edu/Admin/goals/goals.html
Oak Park (IL) Public Library, http://oppl.org/about/library-information/mission-vision/strategic-plan
Southwestern Oregon Community College, http://www.socc.edu/library/pgs/policies-guidelines/goals/index.shtml

CHAPTER 8

Activities

THEORY

Activities or where the rubber meets the road! What your library does, every day, week, month, or year. This is the kind of action that the customers see when they come into your library. These are the actions that your staff does routinely, the individual things that have made your library what it is today and what it will become in the 21st Century.

You might ask, "Why does a strategic plan need to be so detailed as to list staff activities?" The answer would be, "That is the only way to ensure that what your staff does, each individual activity, contributes to the mission." Also, the only way to ensure that library resources are being applied toward accomplishing the mission is to make sure that those are applied to the specific activity that contributes to an objective to achieve a goal. Make sense?

You already know that your staff and their time is the largest resource you have in your library. Just look at your library's budget. Where does most of it go? Personnel. Making sure the staff are being employed effectively doing activities that directly relate to the mission is the best use of your otherwise limited resources. For a better grasp of how valuable this resource is, multiply the number of full-time staff by 2,000. That's the number of hours you have during the coming year to accomplish all that you have planned. It is extremely unlikely you will have more hours, and depending on the circumstances, possibly much less. Every unplanned activity that creeps into your staff's daily routine and takes staff time whittles away at the time available to do all that you want to accomplish. Time is valuable!

The consequence of not including activities in the strategic plan is that you are left with an objective and no planned means to achieve it. This does not mean that your staff, the main resource of the library, has to accomplish everything, but activities are essentially an allocation of this staff. What has to be accomplished to achieve an objective? Who does what? When? How often? With whom? Without the necessary activity to accomplish the objective, the library staff will be left to do their own thing, so to speak, and not do actions that contribute to the mission.

Every organization has employees who prefer to do things they enjoy doing or find rewarding, while tending to avoid doing those things they don't enjoy doing or find unrewarding. It is simple human nature. Allowing employees to determine what they do and don't accomplish will never lead to accomplishing one specific activity leaving your objectives unmet and your goals unreached.

You could ask, "Why not just start with what we actually do? We've been doing the same activities and tasks for years. Are we really going to stop doing circulation, weeding, collection development, or summer reading?" The answer is obviously, "No." However, the reason strategic planning does not start with these common repetitive activities is that, if we did, that would assume:

(1) what we are doing are all of the right or best activities;
(2) all those activities are being accomplished in the best, most efficient ways possible; and
(3) that all those activities actually contribute to accomplishing our mission.

Making these broad, unexamined assumptions negates the fundamental purpose of doing strategic planning. As stated throughout this book, strategic planning is the best method to ensure that your library accomplishes the goals that the entire staff have established to achieve the mission they have determined to be essential. Goals without useful objectives and appropriate activities will never accomplish the mission. The diagram in Figure 8.1 illustrates that relationship.

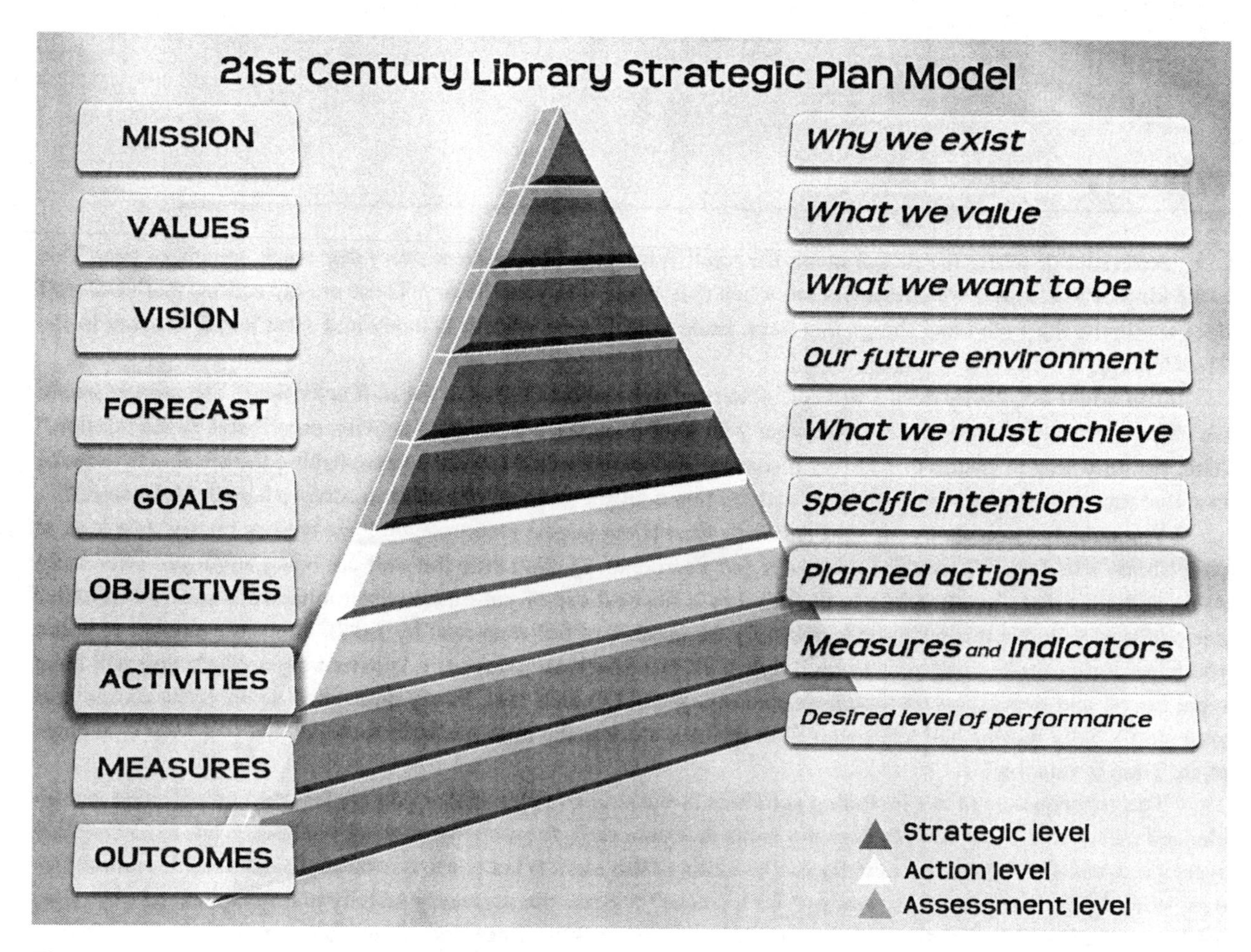

Figure 8.1 Strategic Plan Model—Activities

PRACTICE

At this point in your planning process your staff's and committee's motivation may be starting to wear thin. Meetings that feel like they simply lead to more meetings can do that. People begin to think, "Not another meeting! Don't they know I have actual work to do?" In fact, this is the very worst time for that type of thinking to occur. Why? Because the creation of activities is where your staff will actually commit themselves to tasks that they suddenly realize they may be responsible for actually completing in the future.

Now is your moment as leader to determine the fate of this whole process. You must work to ensure that all the effort your organization has made to arrive at this moment will not falter with the very natural human inclination to shy away from what may seem to them to make them do more work. You must decide ahead of time which of the following two approaches you will use to deal with this predicament. Both of these are reasonable to meet your challenge.

The first approach is one to say, "Yes! We can do it! We just have to give it our best effort and we can do anything!" This approach must also include: "You're right! We all are working very hard already and what we have done here, determining our priorities for the future, may mean we need to let go of some things we are currently doing that do not match our goals and move toward things that do!" If you choose this approach it should be because you believe that your staff truly can handle more (and that they are indeed going to need to continue many of their present activities), or that they are overestimating the weight the additional tasks will have on their work load. If your staff aren't being realistic about any increase in workload, then you will need to provide consistent motivation and explanation as your process continues. Commit to your path and keep going.

The second approach requires more than simple positive affirmation of your staff's abilities. You will need to plan for the process that is necessary to determine which activities currently exist that may need to be tweaked, lessened, or completely abandoned. Realize that this process itself, while incredibly important, may be one of the more arduous battles you face in the planning. People are often loath to abandon an activity in which they have invested time, effort, and resources and still believe to be valuable to the services offered to their patrons.

Consider the scientific study of the chimps. A group of chimps was trained such that when they would climb up a set of stairs to reach a banana, they would be sprayed with water. Eventually the chimps stopped attempting to reach the banana. The researchers added a new chimp to the group. When the new chimp approached the banana the entire group restrained him from reaching it until he finally stopped. The researchers replaced each chimp one by one with a new chimp until the group contained none of the original chimps who had been sprayed by the water. When the researchers added yet another chimp, the group still restrained him from reaching the ladder. None of these chimps had ever been sprayed with water for attempting to reach the banana, but they simply had adopted the behavior of the group. This same behavior can be applied to some of the activities your staff completes. They may not even know why they do them, they just do. These should be the first to be identified and abandoned.

Unfortunately, not all your choices are this easy. You may have to make some tough decisions about activities within your offering as programming, training for staff, special services for patrons, among others. Evaluate, analyze, and review everything that you and your staff do on a daily, weekly, monthly, and even yearly basis. Empower your staff to challenge the norm. Ask them what activity they feel is a sacred cow, which is no longer relevant to your library's mission.

Consider what your reaction will be to your staff suggesting the abandonment of the ultimate sacred cow of programming, the summer reading program. Before you dismiss this idea out of hand, be prepared to listen to the reasons the idea was considered. Do you no longer have a staff member who does children's services? Is the local school district planning some alternative method to help children keep their reading skills over the summer? Is a local bookstore offering some alternative? Be ready as a leader to embrace and carefully consider staff feedback with an open mind. You may find staff will challenge you to loosen your hold on activities you consider as a given, but they do not.

Only you know which course feels right for your organization. You should prepare for this watershed decision and conversations that may challenge even your most deeply held ideas about library service. If you are, then you have come to a place where true change and reinvention of your library into a 21st Century Library is nearly assured. In any case, ponder the issues ahead of time, then choose, commit, and lead!

One advantage to doing good analysis of your library's activities is that you will begin a very rough resource allocation process. People will readily tell you what they think they can accomplish and what they can't. As various activities are being discussed, people will naturally assign it to one or more staff members. This will be your opportunity to assess whether you think they are correct, and whether it is the best solution. Keep track of this informal information for future reference because you will soon be faced with the challenge of resource allocation.

EXAMPLES

Every library staff has its routine activities, one of which is opening the library for customers to come in and be served. Let's assume for the sake of an example that we have identified a weakness in our SWOT analysis and want to improve our customer relations. Our overall goal might be simply "Improve customer service." Obviously, we could accomplish this in many different ways. Again, let's say for the sake of an example that our SWOT revealed a strength in our staff being gregarious and having a cohesive working relationship. It makes sense to apply a strength to remedy a weakness. Let's have our staff interact more with customers to gain their confidence, support, and goodwill in an effort to improve our customer service.

Potentially good objectives under this goal might include the following:

Goal #1—Improve customer service.

Objective O1.1—Open the doors to the library on time every day.
Objective O1.2—Always greet every customer you meet with a verbal greeting and ask if you may help them.
Objective O1.3—Casually observe customers and offer assistance to any who appear to be lost, undecided, or confused, without being intrusive.
Objective O1.4—and so forth.
Objective O1.x—and so forth.

Under each of these objectives we need to develop activities that will implement the objective into actions. Here we enter a common-sense arena regarding exactly how we could do this, and eventually how we can measure the outcomes to evaluate our success (see Chapter 9 "Measures and Outcomes").

Activities

Objective #O1.1—Open the doors to the library on time every day.

Activity #A1.1.1—Schedule at least one employee with library opening authority to be on duty prior to opening time every day.
Activity #A1.1.2—Develop an opening procedures daily checklist to ensure the library is ready for customers.
Activity #A1.1.3—Include opening procedures training in supervisory staff training program.

Objective #O1.2—Always greet every customer with a verbal greeting and ask if you may help them.

Activity #A1.2.1—Include "Library Greeting" guidelines in employee handbook.
Activity #A1.2.2—Include "Library Greeting" training in staff training program.

Objective #O1.3—Casually observe customers and offer assistance to any who appear to be lost, undecided, or confused, without being intrusive.

Activity #A1.3.1—Include customer relations training in staff training program.
Activity #A1.3.2—Conduct peer training exercises to develop customer assistance skills among staff.

Objective #O1.4—and so forth.

Activity #A1.4.1—and so forth.
Activity #A1.4.2—and so forth.

Hopefully, you have recognized by this point that everything contained in the strategic plan is designed and oriented toward achieving the library's mission, everything! Nothing in a strategic plan should be superfluous! If there is anything in the plan that is not an activity that contributes to an objective to achieve a goal, then it should not be in the strategic plan! If it is something you feel is important to the organization, consider revising the strategic plan or putting it in a management plan.

The examples cited earlier are setting up something that will be used as relevant points in Chapter 11 "Organization of a Plan Document." Please notice the logical numbering system to identify each goal, objective, and activity to tie them together. This will associate the parts to each other and the specific goal so that you can keep track of everything under the appropriate goal. At some point you'll find that you have several dozen parts that you may want to interchange when you see them on paper.

DERAILMENT

As mentioned earlier, skipping the activities portion of the planning process assumes that you are already doing all of the right activities, in the best possible way, and that they all contribute to accomplishing your mission as newly written. It further assumes that no other activities are necessary or more appropriate to fulfill your goals. This is a **very bold** assumption, and it is almost certainly not true. If that were true, doing a strategic plan would merely be a paper exercise for your library staff, and you would not need to do anything else. This is extremely unlikely, and you and your staff need to move ahead to complete the process.

Developing activities is actually very near the end of the process, and it would be a shame to lose all that you have gained by allowing any shortcuts to creep in at this point. Sticking to the process will result in exceptional ideas and staff commitment to better activities that will make it more likely that you accomplish all that have been planned and you will have the library you want to have. Remember as has been repeated throughout, people will always look for shortcuts to the planning process. It is human nature.

Up to now your staff may have viewed the planning process as an academic exercise, but now someone is going to have to actually add these specific activities to their list of job duties. When that reality hits in your group you will know it. It will start with a slow realization. You will begin to see it on staff faces. Suggestions and ideas will begin to slow down. Staff will start to look wary and begin to glance around at each other. Then what will happen, someone says it out loud. A hand will go up and someone (you as the group leader may very well know who this is likely to be) will say, "So, I understand these things are important, but we are all already so busy. I don't know how we can realistically add more to our plates." And there it is, the elephant in the room.

Your responsibility as the leader of the process is to guide them through this phase by helping them keep the big picture goal of strategic planning in front of their minds and not allow them to become bogged down into the gloom of creating more work for themselves.

Working through the process should enable staff to see their mission differently, and recognize and understand that their new goals will support their new mission. They have developed innovative new objectives to frame the activities to make it all happen. You cannot allow staff to revert to simply plugging in old activities to wherever they fit best among the new objectives. This would be a waste of a serious amount of valuable time, and you and your staff would probably end up with a strategic plan that is essentially just like the last one. You will have expended significant resources to achieve the old status quo.

What will hopefully happen is that one or more other members of the staff will say something to support the process and suggest the ways new activities will allow everyone to better serve their patrons. If no one does, you need to have these examples ready to share.

SMALL LIBRARY IDEAS

This is the point at which your staff must get intimately involved in the process. No committee or consultant is able to develop activities that will be as practical, useful, or successful except the individual staff member who is performing the activity. If you have been relying heavily upon community input or upon a committee formed of many non-staffers, this is the point where you may want to move into intensive meetings with just your staff. They will have the strongest grasp of how to implement the ideas and vision that has been crafted in the strategic plan thus far.

For example, if one of your goals is to "Improve customer service" and one of the objectives is "Streamline the circulation process for customers," then only your staff will know that a vital activity will be to "Relocate the customers preparing to send a fax away from the area where customers wait to check out their materials." Getting your staff involved will create activities based upon their daily experience serving their customers. Giving your staff the knowledge that you trust them to make these decisions confirms your belief in their expertise with problem solving in a way that you might be less able to do outside the planning process.

CHAPTER 9

Measures and Outcomes

The Institute of Museum and Library Services (IMLS), the federal agency that administers the Library Services and Technology Act (LSTA) Grants to the individual state library programs, defines outcome-based evaluation (OBE) as it relates to their grant criteria. Their website at http://www.imls.gov/applicants/basics.aspx is an excellent summary of what it is and what it might look like.

> **What is outcome evaluation?**
>
> IMLS defines outcomes as benefits to people: specifically, achievements or changes in skill, knowledge, attitude, behavior, condition, or life status for program participants. . . . Any project intended to create these kinds of benefits has outcome goals. Outcome-based evaluation, "OBE," is the measurement of results. It identifies observations that can credibly demonstrate change or desirable conditions. . . . It systematically collects information about these indicators, and uses that information to show the extent to which a program achieved its goals. Outcome measurement differs in some ways from traditional methods of evaluating and reporting the many activities of . . . libraries, but we believe grantees will find that it helps communicate the value and quality of their work to many audiences beyond IMLS.
>
> . . .
>
> **How does a library . . . do outcome evaluation?**
>
> Outcome-based evaluation defines a program as a series of services or activities that lead towards observable, intended changes for participants. . . . Programs usually have a concrete beginning and a distinct end. The loan of a book . . . might constitute a program, since these have a beginning and an end, and increased knowledge is often a goal. An individual might complete those programs in the course of a single visit. Outcome measurements may be taken as each individual or group completes a set of services (a workshop series on art history, an after-school history field trip) or at the end of a project as a whole. Information about participants' relevant skill,

knowledge, or other characteristic is usually collected at both the program beginning and end, so that changes will be evident. If a program wants to measure longer-term outcomes, of course, information can be collected long after the end of the program.

. . .

Example

The following projects' goals include changing behavior and skills through project activities.

PROGRAM: COLUMBIA COUNTY READ TOGETHER PROGRAM

Program Purpose: The Columbia County Public Library, Columbia Regional High School, Columbia County Head Start, and Columbia County Literacy Volunteers cooperate to provide story hours, literacy information, materials, and other resources to increase the time parents and other caretakers spend reading to children.

Program Services

1. Make information visits to neighborhood community centers, County Head Start programs, and Columbia High School parenting classes
2. Provide daily story hours for parents and other caretakers and children at library and other sites
2. Provide library cards
3. Provide literacy counseling
4. Connect learners with literacy tutors
5. Provide children's and basic reader materials to meet individual needs
6. Provide a participant readers' support network

Intended Outcomes: Adults will read to children more often.
Indicators: Number and percent of parents or other caretakers who read to children 5 times/week or more.
Data Source(s): Participant interviews.
Target for Change: At the end of year one, 75% of participating parents and other caretakers will read to children in their care 5 times per week or more.

In the program above, the ultimate goal is to improve literacy in the county, but the project has chosen to measure a more immediate and related goal that provides a short-term indication of progress. That goal is frequent reading to children. Information will be collected through a survey of participants.

THEORY

Measures and Outcomes

Few things explain like a good example. Measures and outcomes may be at the bottom of the 21st Century Library Strategic Plan Model pyramid for a good reason. Without them your strategic plan would be useless. IF you thought developing a useful strategic plan was difficult so far, the real challenge is in these final elements of the process, measures and outcomes. In practical terms, what do you want your library's success to look like? How will you know when you have achieved success? Is 100 percent an achievable level of performance, or 50 percent, or 20 percent? Is your Objective to have 1,000 customers participate, or 100?

The ultimate purpose of measures and outcomes is to determine whether you have achieved your mission by achieving your goals and objectives. It also will show you whether you are actually progressing toward achieving your goals, or whether you need a plan correction to get there. That decision is totally dependent on the measures and outcomes you establish in this last part of your strategic plan, and what the results of that assessment tell you.

While there is still some debate about the value and even purpose of Outcomes versus Outputs, suffice it to say here that the primary distinction is that Outcomes are intended to measure the actual impacts, benefits and/or changes resulting from performance of the activity (What were its effects?), whereas Outputs are intended to measure the raw, objective numbers resulting from performance of the activity (How many? or How much?). In reality, often times both are used by an organization to measure success because both can provide useful information.

Most activities lend themselves to easy measure of outputs, while many are extremely difficult to measure the outcomes, the subjective qualities and benefits of an activity. Outcomes may be the more desirable measure, but they are also the more difficult to determine, but will reveal the impact resulting from the library's activities. Outputs may suffice as a measure of success in some activities, although outputs indicate hardly anything about the changes resulting from an activity, only the amount of activity.

It is your decision as to what measures best provide the management information you need to fulfill your mission. This is another excellent reason why activities are included in a strategic plan, to more easily determine success. Measuring success would be extremely difficult by trying to directly measure an objective or a goal.

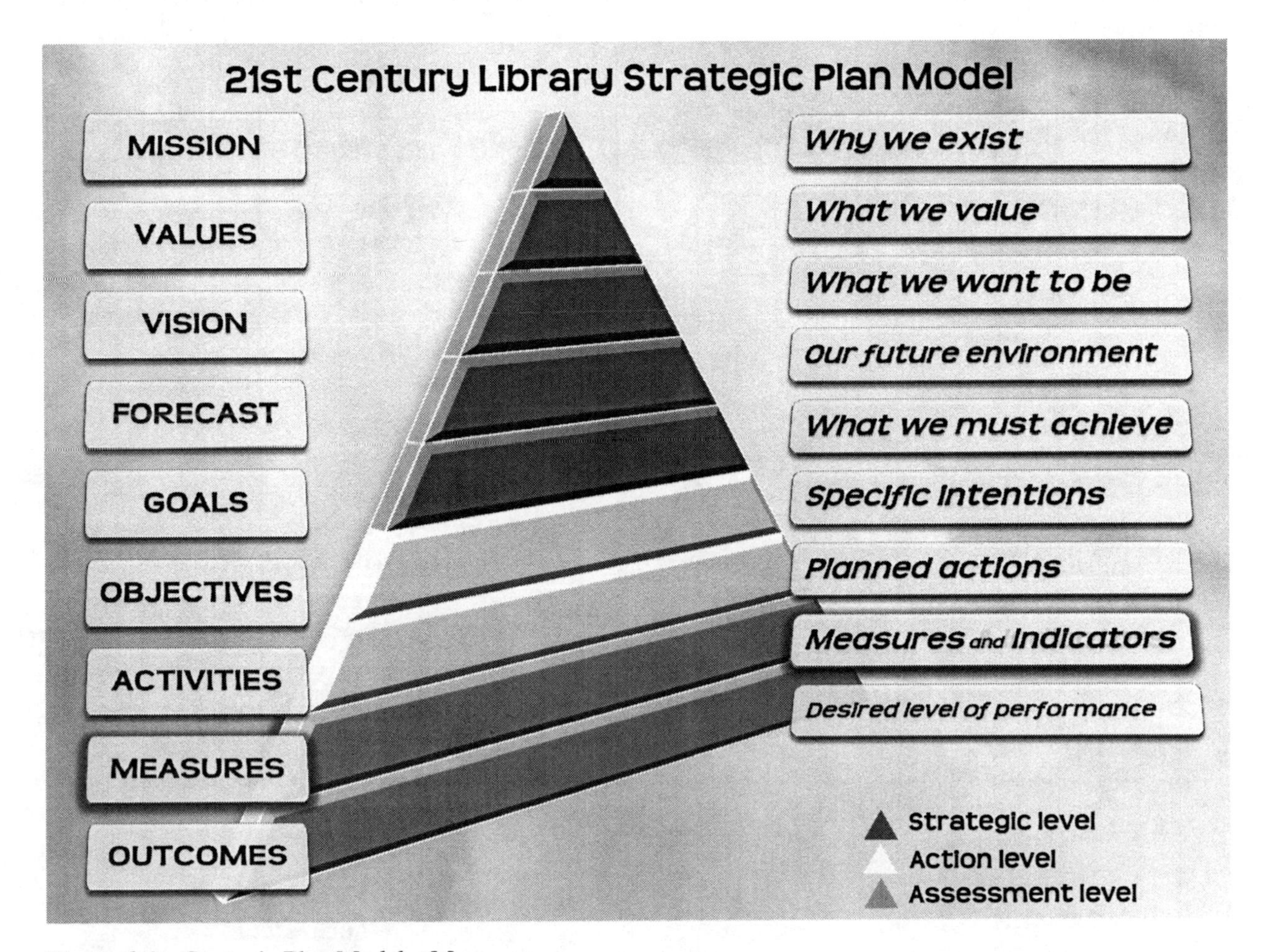

Figure 9.1 Strategic Plan Model—Measures

Measures

As illustrated in Figure 9.1, measures are developed after activities have been identified. measuring the performance of the activity should be determined by using quantitative data. If the results could be plotted on a chart, then it should easily pass a measurability test. Some of the questions that should be considered for developing Measures are as follows:

- What exactly is the Activity intended to accomplish?
- What Measure will best link the Activity to its Objective?
- How will the Measure be calculated?
- What is the source of the data?
- What resources are necessary to collect the data?
- Who collects the data, and how often?
- Will the Measure reveal how well the activity is being implemented or performed?

Outcomes

Outcomes are the next step in the process as described in Figure 9.2. Outcome, as noted earlier, is the actual impact, benefits and/or changes resulting from performance of an activity. Some characteristics of Outcomes include the following:

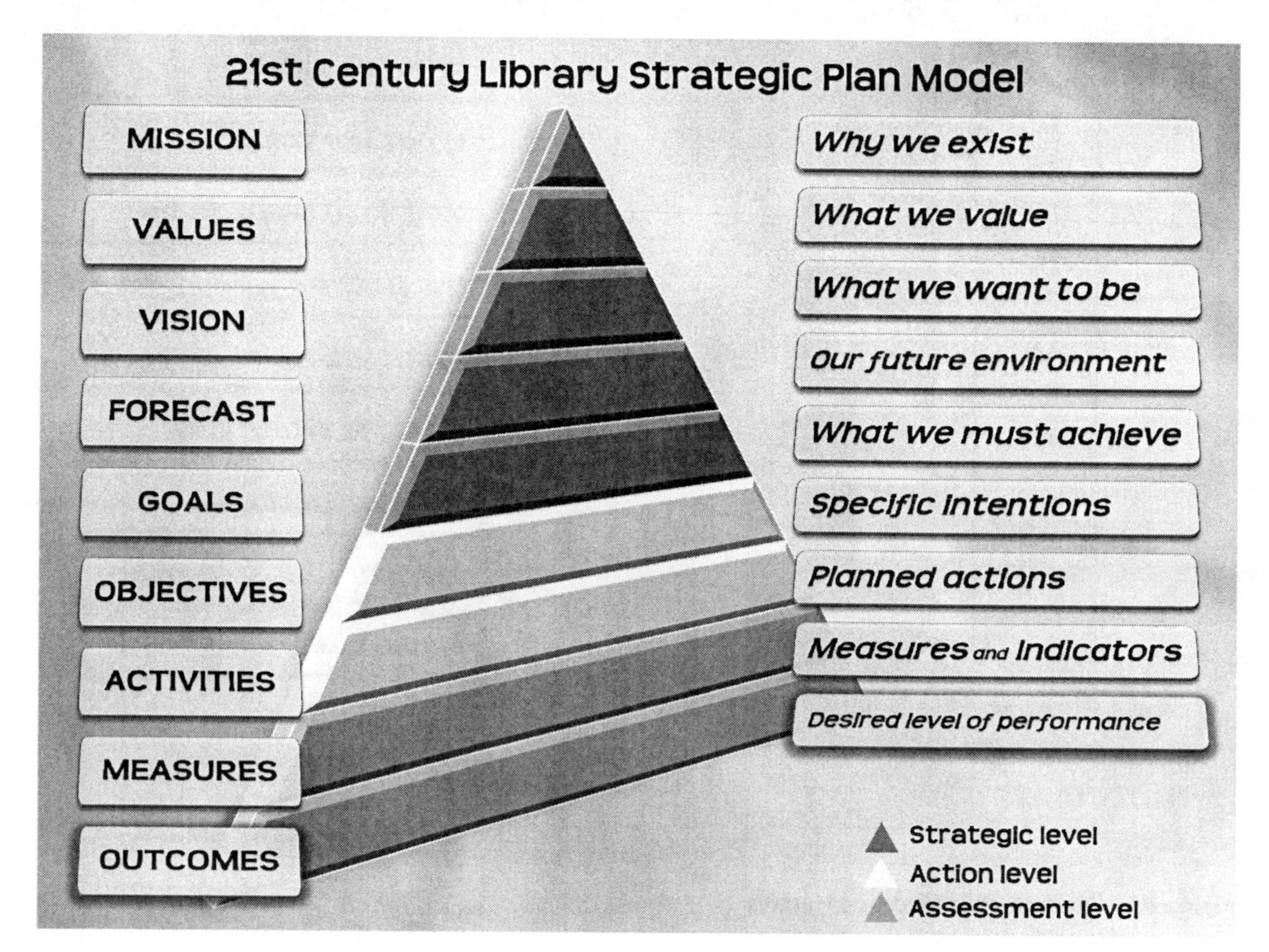

Figure 9.2 Strategic Plan Model—Outcomes

- Knowledge and/or skill *(customers learn to use the online catalog)*
- Change in behavior *(customers actually use the online catalog without assistance)*
- Change in values, conditions, and/or status *(customers prefer to use the online catalog without assistance)*

Targets and Indicators

An outcome also includes targets and indicators, elements by which a measure establishes the determinates of achievement or failure.

Outcome target is the number and/or percent associated with the outcome that you want to achieve (and yes, that sounds suspiciously like an output), because a measure is determining the performance of the activity over time using quantitative data. This is the objective element of an outcome by which success can be determined, whether a raw number or percentage is the basis for determining the level of success, most activities are seldom Pass–Fail, Yes–No, or 0–100 percent.

Outcome indicator is an observable and measurable milestone toward an outcome target. These are what you could see, hear, read, and so forth, that would indicate to you whether the library is making any progress toward its outcome target. This is another excellent reason why activities and measures are included in a strategic plan, to measure progress toward an objective. That would be impossible to determine without measures and outcomes or outputs.

Remember that the whole purpose of measures and outcomes is to determine whether or not you are achieving success in activities. If so, then you are also achieving success in objectives and goals. If not, then you'll need a course correction, and that's where the data becomes critical to tell you what kind of correction.

PRACTICE

As described previously in this chapter, one of the essential, and probably most crucial, elements to this step is deciding who will gather and analyze the data. In some instances it will be extremely logical. For example, if the goal is to increase the access and use of your library's online resources, you may create a design that places the links to the resources more prominently on your website. This activity can be accomplished by your webmaster or IT department. The logical measure of the success of this goal will be whether your usage statistics increase, again most easily accomplished by your webmaster or IT department. In this and many other instances the measurement of outcomes is assigned logically.

Conversely, you may discover that there are areas of your plan that are particularly troublesome and the oversight of measurement and outcome should be monitored by someone that is not as directly involved. For example, if your organization is facing challenges in its relationships between management and staff, if you have been honest in your planning process you will have identified this as an area for improvement and set the appropriate goals, objectives, and activities to achieve this improvement. When the time comes to measure the outcome of success in these particular activities, one can see the inherent flaw in turning to management for that analysis. It may be logical to arrange for a subcommittee of your library board to perform the review, or some other impartial third party.

The one thing that will make much of your planning irrelevant is going an entire year and then trying to collect data. First, it will lead to a time-consuming nightmare, because of the extra time it takes trying to find data that has become lost or unavailable. Second, crunching the numbers will take time you probably can't afford. But most of all, the lack of timely information will prevent making any management decisions regarding any midcourse corrections in your objectives and activities.

There is no set template or formula that can be offered up as an ideal course for the review of measures and outcomes and the declaration of success. You will find as you approach this stage in your planning process that it is just as diverse, unique, and as individualized for your organization as the rest of your plan. The best advice is to keep it as simple as possible, and try to use data collection means that are compatible with your staff member's activities. Contriving elaborate data collection activities will only lead to more frustration and potential bad data.

EXAMPLE

Revisiting our previous Example used with the activities will hopefully provide a familiar scenario to examine measures and outcomes. This example is intended simply to reinforce and elaborate the concepts discussed earlier.

Objectives

Goal #1—Improve customer service.

Objective #O1.1—Open the doors to the library on time every day.
Objective #O1.2—Always greet every customer with a verbal greeting and ask if you may help them.
Objective #O1.3—Regularly observe customers and offer assistance to any who appear to be lost, undecided or confused, without being intrusive.

Activities

Goal #1—Improve customer service.

Objective #O1.1—Open the doors to the library on time every day.

Activity #A1.1.1—Schedule at least one employee with library opening authority to be on duty prior to opening time every day.

Measure #M1.1.1.1—Never fail to open the library on time. (I think everyone could agree that this Measure is in fact a Pass–Fail type of Measure, which is to say that they can be appropriate in some cases.)
Outcome #OC1.1.1.1—Never a customer complaint about the library not opening on time.

(While quantifiable, equal to 100 percent, this would be the time to evaluate whether or not it is achievable, and at what cost. Yet another excellent reason to include activities in the strategic plan, is because you sometimes cannot determine what the impact of an objective will be until you get to the measures and outcome development stage, or even to the final Resource Allocation stage.)

Measure #M1.1.1.2—Never a last minute scramble to find an employee to open the library on time.
Outcome #OC1.1.1.2—Never a customer complaint about the library not opening on time.

(It is not uncommon to have outcomes that are the same or very similar for similar activities or measures.)

Activity #1.1.2—Develop an opening procedures checklist to ensure library services are ready for customers when it opens.

(Note the Activity was revised since the previous example. Continuous revision is common, but caution is necessary to ensure that the changes don't cause a ripple effect that changes an objective or leaves an activity that no longer achieves the objective.)

Measure #M1.1.2.1—Conduct periodic customer surveys to ask about opening on time with full services.

Outcome #OC1.1.2.1—Never a customer complaint that a service was not available when the library opened.
Measure #M1.1.2.2—Conduct occasional spot-checks during library opening to ask early customers whether the library opens on time every day.
Outcome #OC1.1.2.2—Never an employee complaint about the library being disorganized or not ready to open on time

Activity #A1.1.3—Include opening procedures training in supervisory staff training program.

Measure #M1.1.3.1—Conduct periodic assessment of training effectiveness.
Outcome #OC1.1.3.1—Supervisors are able to open the library on time every day and provide all services to customers.

(While quantifiable, "on time every day provide all services," this is another example of time to evaluate whether or not it is achievable, and at what cost.)

Objective #O1.2—Employees always greet every customer with a verbal greeting and ask if you may help them.

Activity #A1.2.1—Include "Library Greeting" guidelines in employee training program.

(Note that Activity #A1.2.1 is now what was Activity #A1.2.2, because it was decided that "Include Library Greeting guidelines in employee handbook" was unnecessary and inappropriate for the staff. This revision only eliminated an unnecessary Activity without affecting the Objective. That's a good thing.)

Measure #M1.2.1.1—Every customer is greeted by at least one employee as they enter the library.
Outcome #OC1.2.1.1—Never a customer complaint about not feeling welcome in the library.
Measure #M1.2.1.2—Conduct periodic customer surveys to ask about helpfulness of library staff.
Outcome #OC1.2.12—Never a customer complaint about not feeling welcome in the library.

Objective #O1.3—Regularly observe customers and offer assistance to any who appear to be lost, undecided, or confused, without being intrusive.

Activity #A1.3.1—Include customer relations training in staff training program.

Measure #M1.3.1.1—Conduct periodic customer surveys to ask about helpfulness of library staff.
Outcome #OC1.3.1.1—Never a customer complaint about needing help and not getting it easily.
Measure #M1.3.1.2—Conduct occasional spot-checks to ask customers whether library staff are helpful but not intrusive.
Outcome #OC1.3.1.2—Never a customer complaint about needing help and not getting it easily.
Measure #M1.3.1.3—Conduct periodic assessment of training effectiveness.
Outcome #OC1.3.1.3—Never an employee who does not know how to assist customers proactively without being intrusive.

Activity #A1.3.2—Conduct peer training exercises to develop customer assistance skills among staff.

Measure #M1.3.2.1—Conduct periodic assessment of training effectiveness.
Outcome #OC1.3.2.1—Never an employee who does not know how to assist customers proactively without being intrusive.

Consider these measures and outcomes examples more of an analogy than a sterling example of a strategic plan, and it's probably an example you could improve. There are numerous good examples available by searching the Internet for what appear to be good strategic plans and then studying them in light of what has been outlined here. Good examples are real examples, but complete examples of all of the elements outlined here are rarely published on the library website. This is appropriate, because beyond the objectives it really is an internal document. The public doesn't really need to know that;

Activity #A1.2.1—Include "Library Greeting" guidelines in employee training program.

Measure #M1.2.1.1—Every customer is greeted by at least one employee as they enter the library.

Outcome #OC1.2.1.1—Never a customer complaint about not feeling welcome in the library.

Every organization should have some internal mysteries about how they do what they do! A simple Internet search of library strategic plan will yield many great ideas from other organizations, even nonlibrary ones.

DERAILMENT

There is a commonly used expression that states: Insanity is defined as doing the same thing repeatedly but expecting a different outcome. Everyone should consider this when developing their measures and outcomes. If you continue to do what you've always done, you'll continue to get what you've always gotten. The only way to change the outcomes is by changing the activities, and concurrently the measures. Traditionally, librarians don't expect any measurable results from their daily tasks, so they usually don't think about measuring them. This is a mind-set that must be overcome.

There are two critical situations that can derail your efforts to effectively determine the success of your plan through measures and outcomes. The first is effective data. It begins with an effective baseline. If your goal is to increase your gate count (the number of patrons coming into your library) in the coming year, then you can only measure that IF your library has been maintaining an accurate gate count for the previous year. Has your counter been working consistently? Have the numbers been being recorded on a schedule? Is your counter a "one-in, one-out" or does it only count once for an in and out? Depending on which counter it is, have any of your employees been dividing the number or recording it as is? These will all determine the accuracy of your statistics. Did your counter break and have to be replaced? How long was it down? Was it replaced with the same type of counter or did your numbers suddenly double? All these issues may seem very basic and something your organization has considered or you may be currently having a forehead slapping moment. The real issue here is that MANY details must be taken into account when you start collecting data. A gate-counter may not even be one of your goals or activities but the basic principle of "the devil is in the details" applies to ALL the statistics your organization keeps.

The second critical situation is to always make sure you are comparing apples to apples, not apples to oranges. Collection and reporting of data may seem straightforward (once the details are ironed out), but anyone who has spent any time collecting, crunching, or reviewing numbers can attest to the notion that they can be shaped and presented in a manner to say whatever you want them to say.

The example was used above of increased use of online resources. When those numbers are reviewed, ensure they are being presented in the same manner they were in the past. For example, if the previous data presented all your electronic resource usage in one number and now it is broken into a different category grouping, this might still work for analysis purposes, but it would be better to have the metrics the same, apples and apples, not apples and applesauce. Otherwise you may have nothing concrete upon which to base the measure of success, because your numbers are not compatible, therefore you may not be able to derive useful management information for decision making. Did we succeed or not? Did we surpass our target outcome? By how much? Do we need to apply more or less resources to that activity?

Last, but certainly not least, as unpleasant as it may be to consider, always remember there may be situations in which the data presented are not accurate. This may occur through innocent human error, or for more manipulative reasons. For example, if you are considering the appropriate allocation of staffing resources into or out of a particular area of service (such as Reference) or department, you may request that the staff keep usage statistics. These might include visits, program attendance, reference transactions, and so forth. To the extent possible, work to ensure that the data presented to you are true and accurate. Human nature and professional ethics can sometimes conflict when staff know that they may be providing the very data that will reduce the staffing in an area of service or eliminate a program to which they are deeply committed. This may present another situation in which you want an independent third party collecting and assessing measurement data.

SMALL LIBRARY IDEAS

Development of measures and outcomes is unconcerned with the size of an organization. However, the reality is still that resources to collect data and analyze the results are highly relevant to a library's size. If you are just a few people, you may lack the expertise as well as the manpower to do a lot of data collection and management analysis. For some of the technology data usage statistics you may have to contact your vendor, webhost, or IT service provider. Where outside resources are used to provide library services, those entities need to be factored into the data collection. Presumably collecting data would not cost additional funds, but you may need to check into the situation to be sure.

Additionally, where staff are limited, or your library organization has no departments, it becomes necessary for a few to do the work of many and data collection may become a simpler task, especially if you follow the advice to keep it simple. The important point, whether you assign data collection to one person or to every individual in their respective area, is to keep up with that task. What this means for your outcomes is that they should be somewhat more obvious than more numerous, in-depth or detailed. An obvious outcome would be one that relates directly to the service that you are trying to measure. If your Objective is to "improve customer service," and your Activity is "get to know more customers," then odds are you will personally experience getting to know new customers, or becoming more acquainted with old customers who have previously kept to themselves. In fact, in a few people staffed library, a routine staff meeting would probably reveal who has gotten to know what customers, and share that information, therefore you'll know the activity is achieved. It doesn't require more analysis than that. So, a simple Outcome that states, "Share information about unfamiliar customers among staff" would suffice for a measurable outcome for your library's purposes.

Taking this simplistic approach to other measures and outcomes can benefit your small library by effectively using the limited resources you have in its most natural form to collect information and analyze the results. In all probability, you have already figured out how to effectively use your limited resources, and this should be no different situation. Continue to think smart.

Be careful not to let time slip away and then try to collect data as an afterthought because that will lead to that time consuming nightmare. Data will become ambiguous or unavailable. Crunching the numbers will take time you can't afford while trying to do everything else. But most of all, any information derived from the data collected will be useless for making timely management decisions regarding any midcourse corrections in objectives and activities.

CHAPTER 10

Resource Allocation

THEORY

Finally, you have a strategic plan that you've developed to accomplish your library mission, laboriously expanded it to include goals, objectives, activities, and even finally developed those good measures and outcomes. Wow! What a challenge overcome, but are you finished now? Not quite yet.

It looks great on paper, but what now? You have to make it work! Unfortunately, the process doesn't get any easier, if anything it may get harder. How is that possible? The old saying that fits here is: "Without strategy, execution is aimless, and without execution, strategy is useless." The last thing you want after all this effort is a plan that cannot be executed to accomplish the goals and thus the mission.

Resource allocation is not one of the elements of the 21st Century Library Strategic Plan Model because it more logically falls within the management plan realm of library operations since everything is accomplished through resources. Resource allocation, the scheduling of activities, and the resources required for those activities, now becomes the lynchpin of your plan. Your plan will succeed or fail based on how well you judiciously apply the limited resources you have available to implement the activities to achieve the objectives and allow you to accomplish the goals you have developed. Resources include anything that could be used in more than one way, over which you have discretion to use as you decide is appropriate including funds, facilities, equipment, materials, and, of course, staff time.

Ideally, all your library's activities have to fit within your budget, even though that was set before your fantastic strategic plan was created. If necessary, the goals or objectives can be scheduled as milestones for achieving over the lifespan of the strategic plan. If it is a three-year plan, then Goal X can be in phases over those three years to be completed at the end of the plan cycle. So, you can spread out achieving your goals for as long as it takes especially if you have to consider a limited budget situation. You can also break them down into subgoals to be achieved consecutively, with, ultimately, the entire goal achieved; whatever works to fit your budget and the goals.

Calculations

In order to determine what you can or cannot accomplish within the next budget year, you will have to allocate your library's resources. One of the quickest ways to begin is to review the current budget and determine where line items align with the new activities and/or objectives from the new strategic plan. Most of your budget is spent on personnel; therefore, comparing those activities and/or objectives that are solely staff driven will reveal where there may be shortfalls.

Within your technology line item, compare that resource with any technology-related activities and/or objectives. Compare all those training-related activities and/or objectives with your training budget. This process results in some serious number crunching by the time you work through the entire plan and the entire budget. Obviously, you have to determine the costs and related resources associated with each activity, because each will be different, and only by itemizing the plan can you derive a total cost in terms of resource requirements.

Other alternative approaches to developing cost estimations are available. If you intend to accomplish everything in your strategic plan, what will it cost? Start from scratch and develop an entirely new cost estimate for each activity and include every cost associated with accomplishing that activity you can possibly think of: personnel, technology, materials, marketing, training, and any others. One of the greatest benefits of this process is that it will also provide you with a future budget proposal when you add into that the remaining fixed costs associated with your library including maintenance, utilities, services, insurance, among others. You will have an estimated budget for the future that is 100 percent associated with your new strategic plan (Hall, Lovallo, & Musters, 2012).

Strategic Objectives	Operating Resources				Timeframe		Funding Source
	Personnel	Technology	Training	Other	Recurring Funding	One-Time Funding	
Objective 1.1	$100,000	$20,000	$1,500		X		Budget
Objective 1.2	$12,000				X		Budget
Objective 1.3		$10,000			X		Budget
Objective 1.4				$7,500		X	Grant
Objective 2.1	$3,000		$3,000		X		Budget
Objective 2.2	$1,000	$25,000	$2,000		X		Budget
Objective 2.3	$2,000	$3,000	$5,000	$2,500	X		Budget
Objective 2.4	$14,000				X		Budget
Objective 3.1		$25,000			X		Budget
Objective 3.2	$5,000	$2,500			X		Unfunded
Objective 3.#	$			$		X	Partnership
Objective #.#				$		X	Grant
TOTALS	$	$	$	$			

NOTE: This is a sample chart intended to demonstrate one way of organizing the Resource Allocation function of a Strategic Plan.

Figure 10.1 Rough Estimate Resource Allocation Chart.

Priorities

Now that you have figured out how much it will cost to accomplish every activity in your new strategic plan, someone may say to you or you may even say it to yourself. "Well, that's not going to happen." Making it happen means you and your staff must set priorities.

Setting priorities is a part of the resource allocation process, and determining what resources for any given activity should take priority over another is a judgment call. Usually, the bigger the cost associated with an activity, the higher the level of responsibility making the decision whether to fund or not fund.

Resources

A rough resource allocation chart may be used to provide a rough estimation of what funding is required, where the funds will come from, and how much funding is estimated for all activities and/or objectives. Figure 10.1 shows a matrix of objectives, activities, and resources allocated by type and an estimated dollar figure allocated in a very fundamental manner.

More detailed charts would include all activities, more precise dollar amounts, man-hour figures, and other applicable quantities of resources.

Resource allocation is very important in implementing your strategic plan. In fact, it could be said that without effective resource allocation the best strategic plan ever developed is no more than words on paper. It would be a tragedy if that happened because of a failure to allocate the resources to ensure activities can be accomplished and objectives are achieved.

PRACTICE

As you begin to look at the different goals and activities you have established in your new plan, it will become clear that nearly every activity will require an allocation of staff time and money. Some will require more of one than the other. It becomes very important to look at the allocation of these resources differently because they require different actions. An allocation of additional staff resources may require a shift as minor as a few extra hours dedicated to a project or as much as actual reorganization of department staffing levels. Budget allocations also come in degrees. While it may be as minor as spending more of your summer reading budget on programming and less on publicity, other activities may require the creation of entire new budget lines and a vote of your board of trustees.

A few primary factors in your resource allocation strategies should be explored. Begin with prioritization as it is the most important and deals directly with how vital any goal, objective, or activity is to achieving the library's mission. Obviously, some of those are more important than others, and prioritizing all of them enables you to be able to cut or delay some activities if your budget is cut. The lowest priority activities are the first to be cut or delayed. Personnel costs are important because, as previously stated, it is the largest single resource in your budget. Allocating personnel costs will help you determine where this resource is being applied. An examination of this will enable you to ensure the right amount of personnel time is being applied in the right priorities. The other costs must be calculated so that they are both accounted for and properly applied to the overall resource allocation.

Prioritization

The usage level of a service is often a determining factor for assigning a priority to an individual library service. Logically, those services that are most used can be expected to receive a larger proportional share of the funds; however, the argument can be made that higher funding might increase use of a particular service. Interestingly, use of services can be permitted or encouraged, but cannot be mandated. Users can influence the allocation of resources in the sense that heavy use of a particular service is likely, although not certain, to result in an increased allocation to that service. Application of the old balance of demand and supply principle usually leads to reduced allocation of resources or even discontinuation of a service where use is lowest. In every case, the library's mission, vision, values, and goals should drive the prioritization process.

Personnel Costs

As mentioned in previous chapters, you will by this point have decided whether or not your staff has the ability to take on additional activities along with their current activities, or if you will need to end some activities. Most likely you will need to make time for those that have been determined to have a higher priority to meeting your mission as defined in your strategic plan. If you have decided you must let certain things go, you will need to ensure that these activities are concluded in a logical manner and that no loose ends are left unresolved.

For example, if your library is maintaining reserve collections at local community centers but you have determined that other activities now take precedent, you cannot simply walk in with boxes and walk out with your collection. You must reach out to those partners and explain your plans to them. Allow them input in the timing and process for the termination of the activity. Work with them to develop the strategy of disbanding the collection. Any project or activity that you have determined no longer fulfills your mission or holds a high enough priority to necessitate the allocation of necessary resources must be ended in a manner that is sensitive to your patrons and community partners. As you move forward, always remember not to burn the bridges you have built.

As you explore the resource, that is, your staff, as leader you also need to keep focused on efficiency and organization. Never fall into the "Well it has to be that way" trap. Do you have your staff allocated throughout your library in the most logical and efficient manner? Are you using people to their strengths? Have you considered the productivity and level of training in all areas of your department? For example, if you have one department that thrives and another that struggles, would it be beneficial to blend some of the staff from one to the other with a goal of strengthening both through training and skill sharing? Is your staff cross-trained? These questions, while a constant consideration for any good leader, are especially pertinent during this stage of your planning process. You may find that through a reorganization, reengineering, and reallocation of your personnel resources, you are able to meet the new requirements of your goals and activities with greater ease. Work smarter, not just harder.

The time may also come when you have to step in and insist that a staff member stop spending time on an activity that the planning process has determined is no longer a priority, even though it is of deep personal interest to that staff member. Depending upon your library policy for working "off the clock" it might be an option to allow someone to continue a project on their own time, in essence, volunteering. That is also a very quick way to determine their true commitment to a particular program or project.

An example of this is related to a dedicated staff member who organized a library's crafting club one evening every month. She spent hours in planning and preparation along with hosting and running the monthly program. When it was determined that the amount of staff resource was no longer justified by attendance and library programming priorities, that staff member was inconsolable and essentially refused to stop the program. Crafting was her passion and purpose. The library director offered to allow her to create her own crafting club and hold her meetings in the library community space. She could plan on her own time, pay for supplies, and create her own promotional material. The staff member quickly determined that her "passion and purpose" was possibly overstated and more likely simply a work task she enjoyed. Problem solved. In the end the few remaining attendees of the craft group actually created their own club and continued to use the library space for their meetings. One could easily consider the situation a win-win.

Financial Costs

As outlined previously, for those activities that require funds, it is important to first look at how much each of those activities will cost. In some instances this will be a simple activity. For example, if you plan to add one additional self-service machine at circulation to your current self-service stations, the dollar amount associated with this goal should be relatively easy to determine with a high degree of certainty. On the other hand, if you do not currently offer self-service circulation and intend to add the service, this number will be much more difficult as there are a great many variables. You may feel you already have the dollar amount from your integrated library system (ILS) provider who informed you a station would cost $x. Have you also considered if that station will require alterations to your facility such as adding additional wiring or moving furniture to make room? How will the new machines impact the traffic flow in your circulation area and will that necessitate any other facilities changes? Something even as minor as adding a stanchion will have an associated cost. Will you need additional signage or multimedia packaging that will work in your ILS vendor's self-service machine, or additional radio frequency identification device (RFID) supplies? The many factors to consider is why this stage can be one of the most difficult.

Associated Costs

In addition to the immediate cost of implementing a new goal or an activity, it is vital that you consider the associated and ongoing costs. What will these associated and ongoing costs be and will there be resources in the budget in the coming years? Also, do any commitments exist with the new activity that will inhibit your ability to abandon the project if an unforeseen complication arises or it is determined that the activity does not have the desired effect toward accomplishing your mission?

An example of this occurred at a small library that accepted the gift of a large garden/park space from a community partner. The library director was approached by the community organization and asked if the organization could create a green space on the library's grounds. The generous gift was immediately, and with much fanfare, accepted and a large landscaped park with wrought iron fencing, beautiful masonry walls, a variety of plant life and trees, as well as several well-placed pieces of sculpture were now a part of the library. After the project was completed, the press conferences held, the ribbons cut, and token gold-tone shovels presented to the library board and director, the realization quickly set in that this gift was not free at all. It would now cost an average of $10,000 annually to maintain just the landscaping. In addition, new policies and security measures were required to maintain a safe environment where previously there were no issues. The library director and board also quickly discovered that no one on the maintenance staff had any expertise in the maintenance of a green space, and they would have to rely on volunteers or negotiate paid-service contracts. In the end, the eagerness to accept a wonderful and generous gift led them to financial obligations they had not considered. This example should be remembered as you approach any program or partnership that initially appears to cost your organization nothing. Everything has an associated cost even if it is just the staff time for planning.

DERAILMENT

As noted in Chapter 1, without good strategy the execution of the plan is aimless; but without good execution any strategy is useless. The most perfect plan is useless if the resources are not properly allocated to achieve each and every activity which will affect each objective and its matching goal in order to achieve your mission. That's the way a strategic plan works. No alternatives are available to allocating resources well and appropriately to achieve the plan. If you don't allocate resources, you might as well not bother to develop a plan.

Therefore, keeping control of the personnel resource is more than essential, it is actually critical. It is the largest resource of which you have control, and it's the one that sometimes and even often trickles through your daily hourglass without accurate accounting. No one likes work plans, but if that is the only way to ensure that each individual on the library's staff is working toward activities that achieve objectives, then you should make sure this happens. Accountability is also not comfortable for many people, but it must be a part of every task. Whatever it takes to maximize the effectiveness of your limited resources is what you should do.

Another easy derailment to the implementation of a new plan or activity is the naysayers who, as a weapon of last resort, will use the sky is falling approach to financial planning of an activity that they do not support. "We can NOT afford this!" and similar cries will ring out. While there are those times when the limited budget is truly a barrier, that decision should only be made after careful consideration of those involved.

For example, if your planning process has determined that your library priority is something as large and costly as a new building, then begin the work to make that a reality. The bigger the cost the more likely it will not happen overnight. If you need a new whiteboard to improve your community space, that can happen overnight. A new building may be a decade in the making, but the decade has to start sometime. If you have determined the need is now, then begin now and do not let the naysayers derail your plan.

SMALL LIBRARY IDEAS

This process should be fairly easy for staff in a small library simply because there are fewer resources to allocate to anything. That is not intended to be humorous, just a statement of fact. The bulk of your budget will also be for personnel costs, so that leaves even fewer resources to allocate.

On the other hand, there are two difficult areas that will require your intense attention: deciding the priorities and human resource allocation. In your new strategic plan you may have developed new objectives and activities that will require more study than usual to determine what resources to allocate for their accomplishment. You may want to seek outside assistance if it is a totally groundbreaking activity for your library. Don't be afraid to go for it.

Undoubtedly, as in the case of virtually all libraries, your most abundant resource is your personnel. It becomes even more critical to make sure that people are effectively used and held to fairly strict accountability to ensure that activities are achieved. Having work plans may be uncomfortable for a small library, but it may be necessary to manage the time to achieve objectives.

As a better alternative where supervision is limited, it becomes even more important for workers to be invested in the organization and self-motivated. Building that kind of team for your small library will net greater rewards than some larger libraries where some staff are simply putting in their time toward routine tasks.

CHAPTER 11

Organization of a Plan Document

THEORY

In the 21st Century Library Strategic Plan Model, Goals begin the multiplicity and development of as many elements as you need to accomplish your mission. Therefore, numbering becomes helpful in keeping track of what goals and what objectives go together. This also facilitates making a matrix of activities and resources for a resource allocation chart by simply using the numbers (Figure 11.1).

For the trainers in the profession, having a resource allocation chart also provides an easy way to accumulate topics to be included in their staff training program. This was the relevant point referred to in Chapter 8: Activities at the end of the "Examples" section. In any strategic plan there will be numerous activities that are related to training. By simply accumulating those activities, the content of your training program is largely complete.

Often times the training program tends to take on a life of its own regardless of the mission or the strategic plan. This can drain limited resources and spend valuable time training on areas that don't directly support the mission. Obviously, if professional development is included as a goal, then that covers a broad range of topics for training. The important point is that training should support mission accomplishment, not just training for the sake of training. Remember, if it doesn't contribute to the mission, library staff shouldn't be doing it.

The generally accepted organization of a strategic plan is similar to the template outlined later. Obviously, many plans exclude the word "statement" after mission and vision, and there are certainly other useful words, such as Declaration of Purpose, Supreme Mandate, and so forth that can be substituted to make your strategic plan as unique as your library. Just remember your audience.

Strategic plans come in as many styles and forms as there are libraries. Finding one that works for you is important because your plan is something that you will use and that will benefit your staff and the library from the

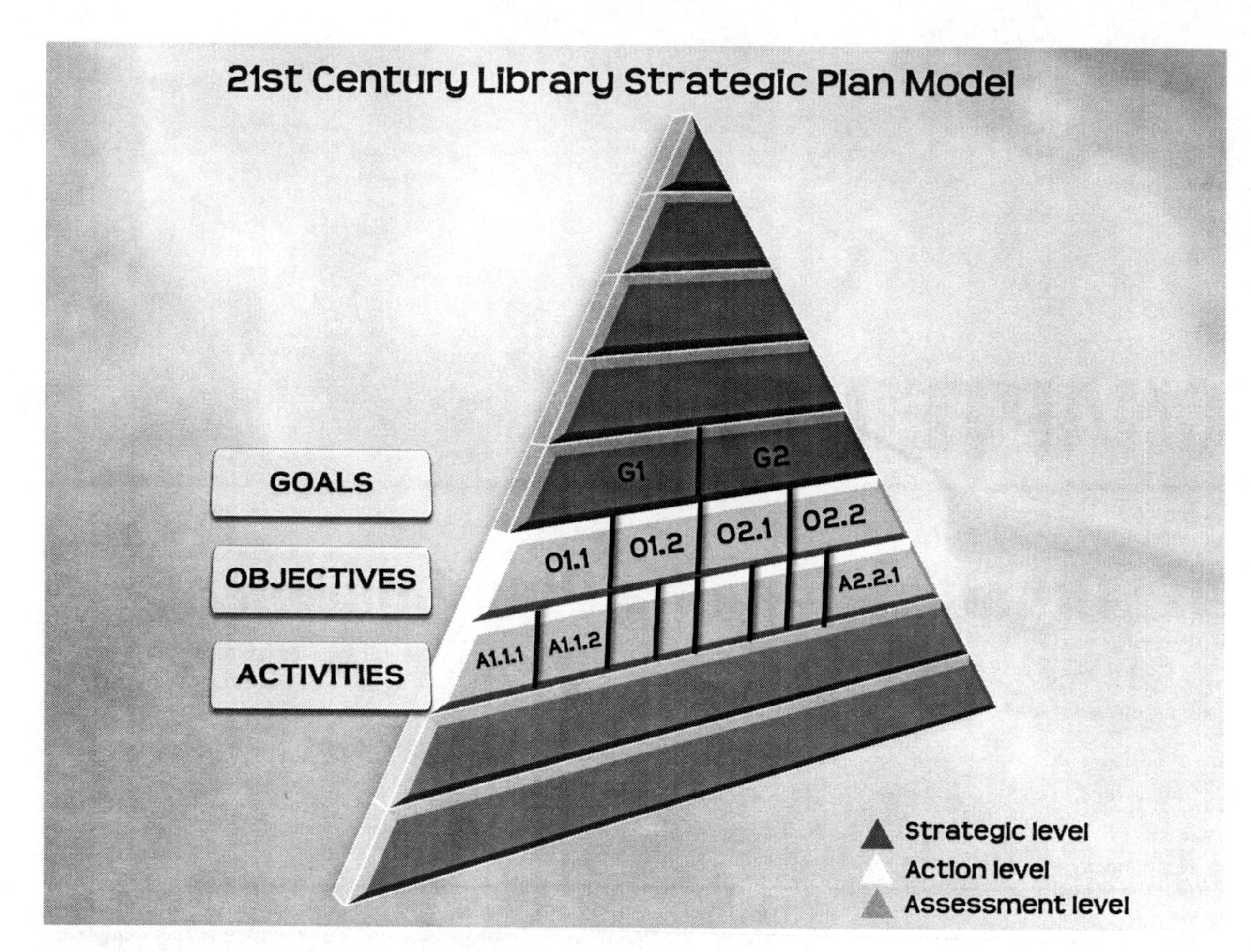

Figure 11.1 Strategic Plan Model—Organization Elements

significant amount of work that went into developing it. Don't hesitate to browse around to find a report format that you really like and can adapt for your library's plan.

PRACTICE

Your strategic plan should, in reality, come in many different forms. Think of your favorite refreshment. It may come in 12 oz. cans, 20 oz. bottles, a 1 liter, a 2 liter, or a 64 oz. mega-drink with a straw, or a 4 oz. juice box. The content is the same but the format or packaging changes with audience and users. Think of your plan in much the same way. You should have a master document that includes all the various components of your plan. This format will provide a jumping-off point for all the other versions. It can be used internally by your administration, board, and any other management agency with whom you need to share this document.

However, this complete master document may be too cumbersome for individual staff, committees, teams, or departments. You may discover that it is useful and more productive to create plans that are group specific. By creating documents that contain all the parts of the plan that are specific to a particular set of staff, that is, department or grade level or position, or other branches for large libraries, you will create documents that are relevant, dynamic, and usable on a daily basis. While all staff will have access to the master document, having a group-specific document will provide documents that staff are really able to use to implement and still feel invested in the whole. When people look at the master document and immediately feel that 50 percent or more is applicable to another group, it is easier for them to dismiss the whole document, especially six months after it was completed.

In addition to these internal documents, you will want to create a public-friendly document that provides context including mission, values, and some factual information about the library (if space permits) in addition to an easy-to-read version of the goals and objectives. Think of this document as another public relations tool for your library. It will allow you to promote your library and its exciting future.

In addition, you may want to consider rewording any goals that are overly laden with librarian-ese in your master document. This does not mean creating a document that has fundamentally altered content! Instead, it is a suggestion that you read your goals from the prospective of a library customer, or even a nonuser and decide if they are easily understandable. Often we forget that the terminology we use daily with little thought such as ILS, Circ, MARC, holds, access point, accession, or even stacks may have no meaning to nonlibrarian staff.

Consider the library who used the term adult videos when referring to all VHS tapes that were not designated as children videos. Seems logical, right? Imagine their shock the day they installed their first Internet filter and were no longer able to access their own catalog. Remember, terminology is tricky and relative. Use wording in your public-friendly plan document that truly is public friendly.

Outside Considerations

Ideally, a library's strategic plan should not be encumbered by outside requirements. Realistically, some states require public libraries to be certified to receive state funding; therefore certain areas are required to be addressed in their strategic plan. This effort ensures that the library is meeting established levels of services to their community. Similar requirements can be applicable to school and university libraries, as well as any other library whose staff must deal with any amount of bureaucracy.

Your strategic plan may be required to include such areas as follows:

- A review of Goals and Objectives for the previous year.
- Goals and Objectives for the next three years.
- A technology component or a complete Technology Plan.
- Public relations or marketing activities.
- Activities for the Board of Trustees to be active advocates for their library.
- Outreach to special or underserved populations.
- Provision for collection, or operations analysis and assessment.
- Plans for grant applications and expectations of grant use.
- Plans for future capital growth.

EXAMPLE

I. Mission Statement—
II. Vision Statement—
III. Values and Guiding Principles—
IV. Goals—

Realizing that the goals area is where you use the forecast information to shape realistic and achievable goals, they should include everything that you want to accomplish in order to be what you want to be. The forecast report(s) should be included in the appendices section.

Goal #1—Improve customer service. (Remember that 21st Century libraries try to break the stereotype of libraries that once served "patrons".)
Goal #2—Use volunteers effectively. (In these times of shrinking resources, this is a highly realistic goal.)
Goal #X—(However many goals you reasonably need to achieve the mission you have framed.)

V. Objectives—

Goal #1—Improve customer service.

Objective #O1.1—Open the doors to the library on time every day.
Objective #O1.2—Greet every customer with a verbal greeting and ask if you may help them.
Objective #O1.3—Observe customers regularly and offer assistance to any who appear to be lost, undecided, or confused, without being intrusive.

Goal #2—Use volunteers effectively.

Objective #O2.1—Recruit undergraduate students from Xxxxx University to become volunteers in the library.
Objective #O2.2—Provide a one-week training program for the volunteers that covers:

a. library policies and procedures, and
b. properly shelving materials.

Objective #O2.3—Evaluate volunteers' performances at least quarterly.
Objective #O2.4—Conduct an annual appreciation event for all volunteers.

Goal #X—

Objective #OX.1—
Objective #OX.2—
Objective #OX.x—

The public version of the strategic plan would normally end after the objectives. It is generally unnecessary to publish for the public the activities carried out in the library or measures and outcomes. These are for internal use to determine whether objectives are achieved. As noted earlier, feel free to change wording and structure to fit a public version of the plan.

VI. Activities—

Goal #1—Improve customer service.

Objective #O1.1—Open the doors to the library on time every day.

Activity #A1.1.1—Schedule at least one employee with library opening authority to be on duty prior to opening time every day.
Activity #A1.1.2—Develop opening procedures checklist to ensure the library is ready for customers everyday.
Activity #A1.1.3—Include opening procedures training in supervisory staff training program.

Goal #2— Use volunteers effectively.

Objective #O1.2—Greet every customer with a verbal greeting and ask if you may help them.

Activity #A1.2.1—Include "Library Greeting" guidelines in employee handbook.
Activity #A1.2.2—Include "Library Greeting" training in staff training program.

Goal #X—

Objective #OX.x—

Activity #AX.x.x—

VII. Measures and Outcomes—

Goal #1—Improve customer service.

Objective #O1.1—Open the doors to the library on time every day.

Activity #A1.1.1—Schedule at least one employee with library opening authority to be on duty prior to opening time every day.

Measure #M1.1.1.1—Never fail to open the library on time. (Everyone could agree that this measure is in fact a pass–fail type of measure, which is to say that they can be appropriate only in some cases.)

Outcome #OC1.1.1.1—Never a customer complaint about the library not opening on time. (While quantifiable, equal to 100 percent, this would be the time to evaluate whether or not it is achievable, and at what cost. This is yet another excellent reason to include activities in the strategic plan, because you sometimes cannot determine what the impact of an objective will be until you get to the measure and outcome development stage, or even to the final resource allocation stage.)

Measure #M1.1.1.2—Never a last minute scramble to find an employee to open the library on time.

Outcome #OC1.1.1.2—No customer complaints about the library not being open on time. (It is not uncommon to have outcomes that are the same or very similar for similar activities or measures.)

Objective #O2.x—

Activity #A2.x.1—

Measure #M2.x.1.1—
Outcome #OC2.x.1.1—

VIII. Resource Allocation—

Resource allocation may be accomplished in several ways including:

- allocation as a broad category or based on operating resources required by category;
- time frame by recurring or nonrecurring; or
- resource acquisition strategy by existing or new source.

A more detailed resource allocation may be accomplished to identify specific budget line items of funds and/or manpower to determine whether adequate resources exist. Charts work well to accommodate the large amounts of information from the strategic plan. Please see Figure 10.1 (page 68), Rough Estimate Resource Allocation Chart in Chapter 10, for an example.

IX. Appendices—

Appendix A—Environmental Forecast Statement
Appendix B—Broad Category Resource Allocation Chart
Appendix C—Detailed Resource Allocation Chart.
Appendix D—Measures Collection Chart
. . .
Appendix X—

The appendices section would include everything that is worth including but doesn't fit within the other sections of the plan outline. This may include the community needs assessment, partnership relationship descriptions, additional sources of funding, funding agency required elements, and numerous others.

DERAILMENT

It would be difficult to be derailed at this point; however, there are some pitfalls of which to be aware. First and foremost is confusing the entire plan with the public version of the plan. As mentioned earlier, the public does not need to know all the magic that goes on behind the curtain at the library. Simply as a practical matter, presenting the strategic part (mission, values, vision, and goals) of the strategic plan is all that is usually required for public consumption. Whether you include objectives is a judgment call. Include those things for the public version that will showcase the bright future and amazing potential of your library!

However, we must remember that as a public agency virtually every document and scrap of paper or electronic scrap, is subject to the Government Records Administration and Management Act (GRAMMA) regulations. By knowing this, you obviously would not want to include anything in your strategic plan that you would not want the public to see. This can sometimes be tough as no one chooses to air their private laundry in public, so avoid putting sensitive library information in the plan in any form.

As you have worked through this process you should have discovered and addressed potential challenges or weaknesses to and in your library. As you prepare these documents for presentation to your board of trustees, community, media, and local government, you may find yourself hesitating to expose those same challenges and weaknesses. Fear not! Draw in a deep breath and recognize that organizations are a living and ever-changing organism. You may have identified some issues that need improvement but that means **you are aware** of what they are and have a plan to change them. Odds are that if you have identified organizational weaknesses, so has your public. They will be happy to see your solutions.

Hopefully, your plan is proactive, and when published you will present issues with solutions. This is your job! This is what leaders do. Wouldn't it be wonderful if there were never challenges or weaknesses in our organizations? Of course, but that is extremely unrealistic. If your strategic plan has identified the needs and developed a plan for improvement, you have done your job well. Now get busy and "do it!"

SMALL LIBRARY IDEAS

Developing a format for the strategic plan report is the same for every size library, simply because it must be reported in some format that is readable by staff, board members, and the public. Whatever format you choose should reflect your library staff and your capabilities. It does not have to be fancy, just understandable. Although, this is one good place to let your library shine, an impressively published strategic plan says a lot about your library. Make it tell the story well.

CHAPTER 12

Choose Your Strategic Plan Ending

We all function in the real world and people have some predictable reactions to any planning process, especially one that embraces change as the 21st Century Library Strategic Planning Model does. Your library has been through a strategic planning process every five years or so because it is expected, or in many cases required. Last time you developed a plan that most people were satisfied with, but for the most part it wasn't used on a regular basis. It was reviewed occasionally, not necessarily annually, and although some things changed during the course of the plan, not even minor revisions were made, certainly nothing major like mission, vision, values, or goals caused you to slightly amend "The Plan." It was supposed to be good for five years, so don't do it again before you absolutely have to.

This chapter develops a scenario based on experience and reality that will help you explore this ubiquitous library endeavor, demonstrate the potential derailment issues, and show you why it should never be routine or mundane. It will also explore scenarios that demonstrate why change is important and necessary in order to arrive at a truly useful strategic plan. If an organization understands and embraces purposeful strategic planning, it can take those steps necessary to create and maintain a useful plan as necessity dictates, not the calendar.

The Road Not Taken
Two roads diverged in a yellow wood,
And sorry I could not travel both
And be one traveler, long I stood
And looked down one as far as I could
....
Two roads diverged in a wood, and I,
I took the one less traveled by,
And that has made all the difference.

Robert Frost, 1920

The poem is well known, but many disagree on whether or not Frost is bemoaning or praising the choice of his path. Everyone has experienced this, the notion that one choice leads to another and before too long those choices cannot be undone nor can you return to the beginning and choose a different route. For good or ill, the path chosen most often sets a new course that leads to a new and unique set of choices that determine your future.

The path of your 21st Century Library strategic plan will be much the same way. It will be a complex series of choices for the leader and the organization, each leading you to another unique set of choices and decisions. It is vital for the success of your plan that, at each turn you make sound choices that will lead to a positive outcome.

This chapter gives you an irreplaceable opportunity to interactively work though the strategic planning process and look at where different choices and decisions might lead. However, unlike in the real world, you can have a do over and change your choices to discover what effect those different choices would have, not only on your process and outcome, but also on the future of your library.

The narrative has been laid out for you in much the same way as the popular "choose your own adventure" juvenile book genre from the 1980s and 1990s. This version is called "Choose Your Strategic Plan Ending." Written from a second-person point of view, as you read you will come to places where you must make a decision which path you will take. These decisions will determine not only probable actions as the story continues, but also the subsequent outcomes. Good luck with your choices!

"CHOOSE YOUR STRATEGIC PLAN ENDING"

As you walk down the hall to your office, your mind whirls over the events of the past 30 minutes. You cannot believe that the library director has chosen you as the chair of the new Strategic Planning Committee! Sure you wanted to be on the committee, but so did all the other managers and department heads of the LaPepperton County Library System. Boy, some people are going to be annoyed when they find out that the director has made her selection and it's YOU.

You regain some confidence as your mind reviews her comments. "I believe you more than any of the other managers or department heads can not only wrangle the different personalities of the people on the planning committee but you also have a unique grasp of planning for the 'profound' . . . of believing we can do what we haven't done before. You will not let the committee and staff get bogged down in the 'realities' of budget, leave that to the board and me, and workload and the inevitable 'but we have always done it like this' that can completely grind progress to a halt. I want to see something we have never done before. I want our plan to look and **be** cutting edge. Not just another cut and paste of our old plans or the best one someone finds online. This is the plan that will take us to the next level."

Her words of endorsement are still ringing in your ears as you enter your department. Staff is busy working on projects and tasks as you head to your office and settle in behind your desk. Now what? The committee has been chosen, the director will send out an email shortly to announce your acceptance of the chair position, and then she wants a cutting-edge plan in her hands in six months. The reality of the task begins to set in as you ponder if it will be a long or incredible short six months.

The jangle of your office phone jars you from your reflection.

"Hey! Congrats!! I just saw the email. So . . . fun fun! The strategic plan is your baby, eh? Wow, I can't imagine what I would want to do less, that or jab my own eye with a spoon! But really that's awesome! You will be great!" says the ever sardonically chipper voice of your best office buddy, Zanna, on the other end of the line.

"Yeah thanks . . . you're a hoot. Seriously I'm excited, but geesh where to start?" you reply.

"Well, I guess you better start with a committee meeting boss! Hoorah!" Zanna says following with an evil laugh.

"Watch it Spicy or guess who I'll recruit to take notes?!" you warn.

"Oop . . . gotta' scoot! Peace!" she tosses out, and before you can reply you hear the dial tone.

Hanging up, you realize Zanna is right and the first step is a committee meeting. So you shoot out an email to the committee requesting suggestions for dates and times that are agreeable to meet in the next two weeks. You hit Send and start an Internet search on "cutting edge strategic plans" and "how to get out of committee assignments if they go horribly wrong."

About a week later you find yourself schlepping an entire copier box worth of handouts into the conference room about 10 minutes before your first meeting of the Strategic Planning Committee. You have printed off everything you can find for the group on innovative planning, effective committee work, and sample plans you thought seemed worthy.

As the members of your committee begin to arrive, you immediately start to read body language to get a sense of the group and what the dynamics will be. First into the room, of course, is Miss Macy. A branch manager, she has been with the library for nearly 40 years and, while wonderful, has very clear ideas of how things should be done and her favorite is "how they always have been done."

Close on her heels is Ellen. She is currently the head of the nonfiction department and tends to be one of your most critical colleagues. She comes right over to peruse the handouts you are laying out and starts "tut-tut-tutting" under her breath.

Next in the room is Becky, a wonderful manager, who is realistic while enthusiastic about change and new ideas. You make a mental note to position her across the room from you, if possible, in an effort to spread the good energy.

Several other various staff mill into and around the room and the vibe is starting to pick up. You are excited and eager to see how things will go with this group.

Next you see Jake enter. Jake, the head of IT is loud, pushy, and does not know nearly as much as he thinks he does. His very presence makes peoples' guard go up as he is a bit of a golden child, somewhat petulant and protected by upper management.

In walks Maggie, a member of the administration. Smart and logical, Maggie is traditionally quiet until she has formulated her position and then, once spoken, you contradict her only at your personal peril. This can be a troublesome situation because she can bring a discussion to a grinding halt if she chooses.

Together the two make an awkward combination for any group and you will need to keep a keen eye on the dynamics as their presence may keep more junior staff from speaking freely. As the last members of the committee make their way in, you encourage everyone to take their seats so that you can get started.

Once everyone is gathered you begin your introduction and pep talk. "Thank you all so very much for being a part of the future of our library! You have all been chosen by our director to assist in this effort because of the strengths you bring. In my conversations with the director, she has made it clear that she is looking forward to this group producing an amazing plan. Something that is unlike anything we have done in the past and will guide our organization into the future!"

"What does that mean?" pipes in Jake.

"Well, that is for the entire committee to decide." you reply. "So, let's get started!"

You begin to pull out handouts and discuss the various stages of the 21st Century Library Strategic Plan Model with the group. You focus on the rough outline of the process the group will follow: mission, values, vision, forecast, goals and objectives, activities, measures, and outcomes. The group is starting to look a little glassy-eyed as you wind down on your explanation of the outcome stage. In an effort to get everyone back on board the planning train, you suggest creating a schedule for meetings and progress.

Almost as if on cue, Miss Macy throws down the gauntlet. "I don't understand why we have to do all this? I have worked on the past seven strategic plans and we usually just have a couple meetings and agree on what we want to accomplish in the next five years, then we write them down and make copies and do it. This sounds like a whole lot of work for something we have been doing fine for decades. And, we always had a strategic plan that worked! So why do all this stuff? We all have busy schedules and this sounds like it is going to take **months**!"

As you hear more than a few of the committee members starting to sound their agreement and numerous heads nodding, you realize this is a make or break point. Do you forge ahead with the new cutting edge plan or do you agree with what is quickly becoming the majority of the group and concede to a more traditional and proven approach? This is your first challenge as chair of the committee, and at this point you must decide how to proceed.

First Alternative Path:

If you agree with the group and opt for the traditional approach, that choice will also get you off the hook for this project. You will be more popular if you go along. If that is your decision, you can jump to Path Z (see page 92).

Second Alternative Path:

If you stay the course and try for the new, the bold, the cutting edge, the more time-consuming, and the plan that is what the director told you she wanted, it will mean a lot of work and probably an uphill battle. You will not be popular. If that is your decision, you can jump to Path E (see page 84).

PATH C

You cannot adequately express your relief that forecasting is over in the planning process and as you look at your outline you smile as you see the next stage: goals and objectives.

"You sound happy!" are Zanna's first words after you say, "Hello."

"I am!" you smile with teeth. "I survived forecasting and now I'm on an easy streak with goals and objectives!"

"Really? Why do you say that?" she questions.

"Because, I don't have to explain this part to anybody! We just sit down, look at what we have done so far and figure out the goals we need to get us there! Easy cheesy!" you practically break into song.

"Truuue. . . . " She says slowly in a tone that makes your smile falter just a tad. "But that doesn't mean it will be easy. Does it?"

"Of course it does!" your confidence refuses to give in. "Everyone knows how to make goals. You just decide where you want to get to, which we have already done, and then the goals and objectives are how you are going to get there! Who hasn't made a New Year's resolution? It's basically the same thing. You decide where you want to 'get to.' Say you want to 'get healthy' so you make a goal to lose weight or go to the gym or whatever. Poof! Goal . . . objective. See!?"

"Uh huh . . . and how many times have you set a New Year's Resolution and actually done it?" she challenges.

"Well . . . " and as your mind rolls over the years and the examples, a sense of dread crawls up your spine.

You consider the multiple times you have vowed to get healthy only to work your way down the fast-food strip like you were playing monopoly and buying up all the squares. Your mind tabulates the dollars spent on gym memberships where the only visit made was their monthly automatic withdrawal from your checking account, or the yoga mat that had only been unrolled once.

"OK well that is sort of fair, but it's not like I'm asking people to plan to work out or change the way they eat!" you retort.

"Your right," says Zanna, "You're going to be asking them to work harder, learn new skills, create new programs, and more! Remember the year you resolved to Learn Italian? How'd that work out?"

Your mind raced back to a particularly frustrating moment standing in the midst of the Stazion Termini in Rome looking over the signage that looked more like ancient Aramaic than Italian for all your time spent practicing with your MP3 player. Your confidence bubble finally burst and you slumped in your seat.

"Thanks for the pep talk. Now that you have me all pumped and ready for the big game do you have any actual usable advice, Coach?" you push back.

"Yes." She says proudly as if this was where she was headed all along. "When people start either making grandiose ideas that you know will never happen; or worse, they refuse to make **any** goals that will actually require them to **do** something, be ready. Know how you are going to handle it ahead of time so that you can come out of there with something useable!"

You start to speak as Zanna continues, "And keep reminding them of the difference between goals and objectives! You may have the goal to be healthy, but the objective is something you can easily determine if you did it or not like 'Join a gym.'"

As she takes a breath you try to break in to no avail, "and then don't you have to go into activities? Yes? Yes! Well the activity might be to take one yoga class each week at the gym and do two aerobic workouts. See?" And you do. Much more clearly than you had when you started the conversation thinking how simple and easy goals would be. "Yes Zanna," you say attempting to keep the condescension out of your voice, "Thank you very much."

"Excellent!" After a long pause for dramatic effect, she continues. "My work here is done!" and before you can say goodbye the dial tone is ringing in your ear. Showy and overdramatic, she is still a great sounding board and you're lucky she's on your side. She saved you from another possible blunder of walking in the room, plunking down in the chair, and saying "Let's make some goals!"

You sigh and begin to type up a simple one-page handout that will provide the group with some examples of the relationship between goals and objectives, and prepare to discuss activities if necessary.

Proceed to Path U (see page 91).

PATH D

After momentarily enjoying the notion of solving this conflict through less civilized tactics, you clear your head, take a deep breath, and realize that this is part of being chair and not everyone is going to be happy all the time.

You say with true sincerity, "Clearly you are really upset. I'm sorry for that. Help me understand what the concerns are so we can work to change the situation."

Pausing for a moment, Ellen clearly didn't expect such openness to her complaints, and she continues indignant but with less edge, "WELL, in the meetings it just seems like you are picking and choosing which ideas are going to make it into the plan! And . . . well . . . That's not right!"

You speak slowly, choosing your words carefully, "I understand what you are saying and I'm very sorry that you felt I did that. It was not my intention. I was simply trying to—"

"And here come the excuses!" she geared back up.

"Nope, no excuses." You begin to try again picking a new route through the verbal judo. "While I was listening to everyone brainstorm ideas it seemed really clear that some fell naturally into slots in the plan, the mission, the goals, and objectives while others just . . . well . . . they didn't seem to have a home or place to land. Does that make sense?"

"Not in the slightest," Ellen huffed, nose slightly in the air.

"Well, let me rephrase. While we are brainstorming, some of the ideas create a pattern and go together. For example, we have the goal of improving patron access to circulation. People have made a lot of really good suggestions that do that and will help us reach that goal. Then we have other ideas, . . . " I began as I carefully searched for an example of one of my ideas or someone else's she wasn't a fan of, " . . . like the coffee shop idea. Everyone seems to like the idea generally, but where does it go? The activity doesn't support any goal, objective, or solve any areas of concern we identified in the forecast. So it didn't 'land' anywhere."

You stop speaking to search Ellen's face and see how your words are settling. She seems to be listening and so you forge ahead. "If the idea fits with others, then we can find a place for it in the plan. If it doesn't then it doesn't mean it's a bad idea, it just means it won't help us reach our goals so we probably shouldn't spend the resources pursuing it."

You can see the internal struggle Ellen is having. She thought she had cornered you being arbitrary and purposely excluding people's ideas. Instead, it appears you have convinced her of your sincerity and the rationale behind your actions.

"Well I still think some of the ideas were really good and I hate to see them set aside. Maybe we could at least reconsider a few of them." She says, clearly on the downhill slide of her argument.

You say, "I agree! How about if I make a list of all the ideas that didn't find a home and present that at the next meeting? That way we can see them all in one place and revisit whether or not they should indeed be included?"

With that you take the remaining bite from her bark. "OK, that sounds good." She looks at you for a moment, appearing to struggle with something else she would like to say. Deciding against it or simply deciding to hold it for another time, she turns and walks out of the stairwell.

You breathe a huge sigh of relief realizing only then that you have been gripping the files in your arms until you are white-knuckled. You loosen your fingers and shake them a bit as you turn to head to your office.

First things first: Breath. Second: Make good on your promise and make that list.

As if confronting an old foe has been your last large hurdle of the process, you and your group sail through the next few meetings finalizing your activities and moving on to measurements and outcome. Thankfully, your library staff has always kept great statistics and you identify which ones will continue to be relevant and will specifically apply to measuring the success of this strategic plan. In addition, your group works through the plan and for each objective and activity you define a specific outcome and target that will determine success.

Now that it is time to incorporate the real-world issues of resource allocation it is time to present the plan to the management team for review and tweaking, and as unnerving as this step may feel, it's time.

Proceed to Path M (see page 88).

PATH E

So you have made the decision to push forward into the brave new world of 21st Century Library strategic planning! Good for you! This is what your director asked for and this is the path that will help you create a plan that has more meaning and value to your organization.

"Miss Macy, I completely understand what you're saying and you are completely right that this will be more work and take longer," you intone. You add the compliments you hope will soothe her sense of tradition and that she has brought up a valid point. Hopefully, the compliments will convince her that you understand and respect her experience and perspective.

"I am simply doing as our director has asked. She is confident that this group has the perspective, experience, organizational memory, and profession astuteness to create a plan that takes us to the next level! A plan that will allow us to take all the great work we do every day and our spirit of innovation and present it to the public in a way that really showcases what we do and who we are. Not just the plans that have been our standbys in the past. She believes this group can create something more impressive. I hope we can all work together to build this through this process because I'm not sure any of us individually know exactly what it will turn out to look like!"

"Well I think it sounds exciting, and I was getting a little tired of the same ol' same ol'. Count me in!" and with that comment from Becky it's as if a spell breaks and more heads begin to nod their agreement and approval.

Not wanting to allow the positive energy to dwindle for even a moment, you chime in "Fantastic! Well, let's get this schedule going" and the group quickly begins to outline a timeline for the next six months for the various stages of the plan.

Back in your office after the meeting, you breathe a sigh of relief. Something tells you that you managed to circumvent disaster and are headed down the right path for now. Just as you reach for your purse prepared to call it a day, the phone rings.

"Sooooo, I hear you are the new be-all-end-all guru of strategic planning?!" snickers Zanna over the phone line.

"UGH. Cut me a break! This is going to be tricky enough. You're sure you don't want to be on the committee." you say.

"Not a shot! I would miss out on all the fun of being in the peanut gallery," she laughs. "But seriously, I did hear it went well. So now what?"

"Well, now we start working our way through it step by step and trying to keep everyone motivated and going in basically the same direction," you respond.

"Our ships must all sail in ze zame di-rection!" Zanna bursts with a thick German accent. She knows quoting movie lines always cracks you up.

"HAHA! As long as I don't wake up with a horse's head in my bed, we will be just fine!" you laugh as you hang up the phone.

Over the next month the committee meets twice to begin the process of brainstorming mission and values. The process seems to be going well and your updates to the director are met with approval.

Continue on Path F (see page 85).

PATH F

At the second meeting discussing mission statement the discussion is rolling along. The group has torn apart the current mission statement and is working on determining who the organization is now so that the wording of the new statement will meet with everyone's ideal of who the organization is now.

Just as you feel the group is beginning to put the statement back together in a fairly cohesive way, up pipes Jake "So, are we done with this yet?"

All eyes of the group turn nearly simultaneously toward the words that, with their impact have deflated all the energy in the room like a bucket of cold water.

"I mean really, this isn't rocket science, people. It's a sentence! Don't we think we have beaten it to death at this point? Can we call it good and move on?" Jake intones in something that is awfully close to a whine.

"Well, frankly, I don't like what we have so far! I'm not even sure it's a complete sentence let alone a "Statement" of who we are" states Miss Macy with resolve.

"Geesh, Jake, you have a hot date or something?" Ellen jokes trying to lighten the mood which has darkened quickly.

"No. But I do have a lot of work to do back at my desk, and if we are going to hash every word of this plan the way we have done this 'statement' we are going to be here all year!" Jake stabs back.

Before it can get any more heated you step in, "What I hear is that some of you feel we are not yet there with our statement and others do." This statement is met with a serious eye-roll from Jake but you forge ahead, "So let's make a plan. We will continue to discuss it for the remainder of this meeting which is only another thirty minutes or so. When we finish we will have hashed out two versions of our statement. We can then all ponder them between now and the next meeting. Then the first item on the agenda for the next meeting will be to pick one of the two and move on to values and vision. Does that work for everyone?" You look around the room hopefully. The group gives its approval and the meeting ends rather productively with two viable candidates for the mission statement.

As you ponder what has transpired you realize that you are going to need to work harder at guiding your group. You know that you don't want to turn into the driving force. You have been on committees like that and in the end the product is usually just the creation of the chair. However, if you do not provide enough guidance and help the group in the process of building consensus, nothing is ever going to get done. You have been on committees like that as well and nothing is more frustrating than going to meeting after meeting where all you feel like you are doing is spinning your wheels.

What you had not realized up until now is that the difference between those two extremes has been the chair of the committee providing guidance, focus, and nudges when necessary. You will need to find methods of guiding the group without sabotaging the organic creation of ideas bigger than any one individual. You also want to create an environment where consensus builds naturally because no individual feels trampled or unheard, but rather a part of the process.

As the leader, it is going to be up to you to know when the goal has been reached and convey that to the whole group, or recognize when you have reached the group's limit of productivity. You must also be able to decide when further work would be less productive than the group has already produced and stop. And you will need to be responsible as you move forward for setting clearer mile markers for progress. You do not want to hear from anyone again, "Are we done yet?"

Vowing to use this approach starting at the very next meeting you feel your own sense of productiveness. Time to get prepped.

Proceed to Path R (see page 89).

PATH G

Well, try as you might and with every good intention, you have fallen into the uninspired path of strategic planning. You proceed through the remainder of the steps quickly and just as uninspired.

On the upside, the plan is finished. Your task is complete. Your library has a new strategic plan. Unfortunately there is nothing new or cutting edge about it.

You watch over the following weeks as the plan is presented to the management team and the staff by the director with as much enthusiasm as she can muster . . . which frankly, isn't much. In your next meeting with her the disappointment is palatable.

"Well, I won't pretend I'm not disappointed. I really thought you were the person for the task. I really thought you would take the possibilities of this moment and run with them. I guess I was wrong about you. And unfortunately it's the library that loses."

The director sighs heavily as she leans back in her chair. In the ensuing silence you realize your showing with this assignment has forever changed your path within this organization. Somewhere deep in your mind, you hear a soft beeping begin that sounds like some kind of countdown . . . that can't be good.

The End

If this is not the ending you want to settle for, go back to the end of Path O to take advantage of your "do over" by taking the other Alternative Path, Path T (see page 90).

PATH H

Feeling somehow like you have avoided disaster, even if it did involve adding at least two additional months to the schedule, you glance out of your window as you consider the next step in the process. Vision. Great. Some days it feels like all you can do just to get through the tasks at hand let alone be visionary. How on earth are you going to inspire the committee to create a vision? You pick up the phone and punch in Zanna's extension.

"Howdy Chica!" Her chipper voice indicates she has noticed her Caller ID.

"Hey, so . . . I need to be inspiring. Thoughts?" you jump right in sounding anything but inspiring.

"Well, you know I have my handy dandy little file of inspirational quotes I can send over . . . I think I may even have a book you may be able to use . . . something about 'Timeless Quotes for the 21st Century' or something like that. I will look." Zanna offers. You can hear her voice trailing off as thoughts of what she could send your way filled her brain.

"OK, that sounds great. I just really want to inspire them to think outside the box about this vision statement and see if I can get something really wonderful going" you sigh, sounding a little less than hopeful.

"Alright. Well, I'll send it over!" Zanna sings as she hangs up.

After the last meeting and the sour note about participative management you want to make sure that this meeting is really upbeat and positive. This is the time for people to be thinking about what the library and the profession *could be* if you all lived in a perfect world. All the negatives like budget and reality of resources can come in later, but for now; this is about dreaming.

You walk into the next meeting feeling great. Armed with Zanna's inspirational quotes, a couple of great movie clips about librarians, and a few stories of great library moments you have gleaned from other staff, you are ready to inspire!

Proceed to Path O (see page 88).

PATH J

You can do this!! You have confidence in yourself just as the director did and you will make sure this goes off without a hitch.

You methodically plan your approach to the forecasting step of the process. You turn to the Internet and begin to print everything you can find on STEP and SWOT. You find a wealth of information and various sample exercises you can do to help the group work through the process. In addition, you print organizational statistics on everything from circulation to gate count and web visits to a decade's worth of budget numbers. You have everything the group may need to plan for the future.

You confidently stride into the next meeting pushing a book truck loaded down with handouts on today's topic of Forecasting using STEP and SWOT. As the group filters in, energy is high and things are looking great. Everyone begins to take their seat and so you begin to talk about forecasting and today's agenda as you begin to have the group pass around the handouts.

As you come to the end of your piles from the book truck, you look around the room. Committee members each have a pile approximately an inch and a half thick in front of them and most are leafing through. Nearly finished with your introduction, you start to see the subtle glances between group members. The glances turn from bemused to nervous to downright panicked as they work deeper into the pile.

You forge ahead and begin to highlight the different statistics you have gathered for the group to review as they begin to forecast. You now notice that some have stopped reviewing the documents and at least two members of the group have pushed them back on the table and have leaned back in their chair. The energy level that you first felt when the meeting began is long gone and has been replaced with a sense of desperation, frustration, and irritation. Those group members not experiencing some form of " . . . tation" have simply tuned out.

All too late you realize that you have doomed this forecast step in the process. The group has become hopelessly bogged down in the how-to's of the exercise and the probability that any constructive thoughts and ideas will be created is nonexistent. You now feel the same sense of detachment you see in the glazed eyes of your committee members as you look about the room. You work through the steps of your process producing stale, cardboard ideas. But, frankly you feel grateful that anything came of these stupid exercises. Whoever decided forecast was a good step in the process deserves a punch in the nose! You are simply grateful that part is over! Why do you feel on the edge of survival?

Proceed to Path G (see page 86).

PATH M

Your committee has done all it can do and now you find yourself with a final draft. You submit it to the management team for their review and recommendations. After receiving those, your group meets yet again and tweaks the final product for submission to the administration, the board, and the financial officer of the organization.

The director couldn't be more thrilled. She gives praise openly and freely to your committee and the staff as a whole for creating a product that will lead the organization into the next three years.

This is where the rubber meets the road. For all the planning and thought that goes into such a plan, its success hinges upon the allocation of resources to make it happen. The director, board, and financial officer look at the associated costs of all that you and your committee have determined are the goals for the coming years. The director calls you into her office to discuss the plan.

"I wanted to let you know what a wonderful job you and the committee did. I know it was a tremendous amount of work and I know there were a few rough patches. I wanted to tell you personally that the administration and board have determined that all of the plan will be funded. For a couple of big ticket items like the self-checkout system, we will be extending two more years before we fund it, due to budget constraints, but it will happen. You and your group really did such a great job not only identifying the issues facing the organization but creating a plan that addresses those needs along with adding services that really drive us into the future. Because of that effort, everything in the plan was an easy sell to the board and will be to the county commission as well when we approach them for increased funding. I really couldn't be more pleased. Great job!" You nearly float all the way back to your office and have barely settled in your chair when the phone rings.

"Hey, Hey, Chica! I just read an email from the director that very nearly gushed out of the computer monitor. Actually, I think I see it dripping a little! HaHa! So she says it's all done and it's great." Zanna pokes you in good natured fun, but nothing can deflate your happy balloon in the slightest.

"Yeppers! I just met with her. They are going to fund it. They love it! They love me! And I love you for all your help my friend. And I . . . well, I am so happy it is all over!" you release, as you lean back in your chair realizing the truth of your words.

"Any time! And Wow! I bet you are glad it all finished up. I have barely seen you in the past nine months. I feel like we only ever talk on the phone! So first lunch is on the agenda and then . . . what are you going to do with all your spare time!?" she asks.

Smiling, you reach over and grab the book sticking out from under your purse and, as your eyes rake over the cover, Michelangelo's David and a head shot of Rick Steves smiles back at you. "Me? I'm going back to Italy and this time . . . well, this time I will know how to ask which track the train to Venice is on!"

About 10 seconds after you hang up reality creeps in and you realize that the director is going to need somebody to follow this new strategic plan and make sure it gets implemented. Did you shoot yourself in the foot by doing too good of a job? No. It's your baby and you're going to make sure it lives a long and productive life.

The End

PATH O

The last committee meeting could not have gone better. The group worked together and created a vision that was truly inspiring. They did not get distracted by the realities that can exist in day-to-day library business, and instead really embraced the moment to dream and create. You can't help but feel your efforts to create an inspirational environment were a part of that success. Now, if you could just capture that again in this next step . . . the forecast.

This is certainly a part of the planning stage that you have been dreading. Sure the other parts have their potential pitfalls but, honestly, this part is just a bear technically. You have done all the research and been part of using these tools before but frankly they still stump you. In your research you read somewhere, "Simply put, the forecast uses the facts of the present to determine what is most likely to occur in the future." HAHA . . . OK Sure that sounds great. But, when you are chair of the group and it's up to you to get a whole bunch of people working together to decide what is likely to occur in the future it doesn't feel so simple. So yes, you have these handy tools or exercises to use to do it: SWOT and STEP. They just seem very complicated to you. Breaking all the ideas down into the different categories and then how they relate to the internal or external environment, puzzling. Even just pondering it sitting here at your desks you start to get the acronyms confused.

As you ponder how you will approach this step with the committee, you consider the pros and cons of approaching the director for advice. On the one hand you know it is entirely likely that she will have some pearls of wisdom for you, on the other she likes to know that her managers are capable of handling situations and not always needing to run to her for advice.

First Alternative Path:

If you decide to forge ahead and not risk looking needy to the director, proceed to Path J (see page 87).

Second Alternative Path:

If you decide that it may be best to seek the director's opinion rather than risk a blunder, proceed to Path T (see page 90).

PATH P

Really? REALLY?! Oh, now come on! You know this wasn't really an option! Yes, the planning process can get tough, and yes, sometimes you will be underappreciated and even take the brunt of other's frustration, but resorting to violence is never an option! Throw her down the stairs? There is a reason this was path P. It's called Prison! Shame on you! Stop indulging your fantasies, and . . .

Proceed to Path D (see page 83)**.**

PATH R

You begin putting your new approach to work immediately at the next meeting!

"So, we have all had a chance to live with, ponder and sleep on the two mission statements we created at the last meeting. Are we ready to choose one and move forward?" you pose.

Much to your relief the group reaches nearly immediate consensus on the choice and you are ready to move on to values. The discussion is making excellent progress and the group has identified most of the obvious values such as excellent customer service, fiscal responsibility, and so forth. You are feeling great about how the group seems to all be on the same page and this part of the process may whiz by without needing much discussion when Becky chimes in.

"Well it seems to me that we haven't yet included one of our most important core values, participative management and open communication!" she states.

As heads begin to bob up and down, you hear a strangled guttural sound coming from Jake when you realize he is doing something between choking and laughing.

"Excuse me? Was that funny?" Becky asks.

"Well only if you were being serious! You say that like you drank the Kool-Aid. I mean, you know that isn't really how most staff feels that it is around here. Don't you?" said Jake, sounding more serious and sincere than before.

"Absolutely not! We value staff input. We are always sending out all staff emails asking for suggestions and participation and letting staff know that we want them to be involved!" rebutted Becky, still clearly defensive of her position.

"You're both right," another committee member jumped in, "and wrong. As an organization we say all the right things and ask staff what they think. But then what happens to the input? Most staff members, in general, feel like 'why bother' because they know it's all lip service, that nothing will come of their suggestions."

"That's not true! I implement staff suggestions all the time in my department!" countered Becky.

"I'm sure you do; but that doesn't mean that everyone does. And a lot of staff is a little sore about it! Let's just say the opinion of 'participative management' isn't the same from every chair in the organization!" another staffer stated.

Suddenly it seemed everyone had something to say and the jumble of voices soon became a cacophony as opinions and strong statements filled the room. What has happened to your calm productive discussion? In the blink of an eye an issue has been raised that could change everything. Or it could be that this is simply an isolated perception or personal agenda that is surfacing in the discussion with the dynamic of the players in this room. You as the chair have to decide how you will handle this issue.

You quickly make the call that perception and reality are closely intertwined. Even if it is simply the perception of the staff that the management and administration of the library are not listening to them, that will be a large problem for the strategic planning process. It is vital that all members of the organization feel involved and valued if a cutting edge 21st Century strategic plan is going to be created through this process. It is a daunting enough task without having a significant number of stakeholders feeling disenfranchised.

You liken it to moving a piano. If you are attempting to move a piano, that is a difficult enough task without having any impediments to the move. Say in your house, you have a loose stair board. During normal daily use it may creak or shift slightly, but now that you put that stair board under stress with the weight of piano and movers, what is normally just a groan now breaks under the added stress. It stymies the entire process of moving the piano. You feel this issue may turn into the same. General groans from the staff on a daily basis may, under the added stress of strategic planning, turn into a more destructive process causing a break in communication.

You determine that this will need to be addressed not only in the plan by way of goals and activities geared towards improvement, but also during the process. Your planning committee will need to strengthen their efforts to involve staff in the planning in a meaningful way that lets them know they are being heard and that their input will have an impact upon the final result.

As your mind has been whirling, the group chaos has wound down a bit and people are beginning to look at you for something. You share your thoughts with the committee. This leads to a more productive conversation about including staff in the process. Although it will add time, possibly months, to the planning it is determined that a series of town hall meetings should be held with staff to generate discussion and ideas on organizational areas of concern that will be addressed in the final plan. To insure that staff feel heard, the ideas generated by each town hall meeting will be compiled into one mass document that is disseminated for all to review. Staff will be able to see a direct correlation between issues raised in the town hall meetings and the goals of the final plan.

Satisfied that you have cleared a significant hurdle that could have, if left unaddressed, derailed the entire process, the meeting adjourns with a good vibe from all members. Good work!

Proceed to Path H (see page 86).

PATH T

"I really am not looking forward to this next step in the planning process, the forecast. It just seems so complicated and as if we could really get bogged down in the process and not come up with really great ideas! Heck, I get confused enough trying to keep SWOT and STEP straight that I sometimes feel like I'm going to have to write crib notes on my hand!" you laugh nervously as you lightheartedly raise your concerns with the director.

She laughs, "I know just how you feel! That has never been one of my favorite things. But they are effective and that's why we use them! Well whatever you do, my advice is **do not** walk into the room and say 'Hey, guys, so today we are going to forecast using SWOT and STEP!' That is a surefire formula for getting an entire group of people to completely shut down. The folks who know the process will groan and those who don't know it will glaze over somewhere during the intro! Do yourself a favor and approach as a series of questions such as 'Today we are going to talk about our organization's strengths and weaknesses' and 'What opportunities and threats to our organization, services, and profession to you believe exist?' Brainstorm the discussion and then you work the feedback and ideas into the SWOT and STEP later."

Just like that she had dropped the solution into your lap. You experience a sweep of relief and know that you made the right call asking her opinion. Otherwise, you would very likely have gone in with oodles of papers defining STEP and SWOT and attempting to work methodically through the exercises after explaining them to the group in detail. Who knows what would have resulted!

It takes three group meetings in total to work through the forecasting process and once completed, your group has defined a cohesive picture of the opportunities and challenges facing your organization both internally and externally that will have an impact and should be addressed through the strategic plan. It's time for goals and objectives, so . . .

Proceed to Path C (see page 82).

PATH U

The process of creating goals and objectives went swimmingly thanks in large part to Zanna's advice. And, the committee has sailed into the activities creation stage easily. You just finished your first meeting on this subject and you think you will likely have one more before you are ready to head on to the next stage; then it's clear on to sunrise!

You are soaking in the mental sunrise of the finish line as you notice that Ellen is hanging back in the hallway clearly waiting for someone to leave the room. Geesh, you hope it isn't you . . . that is really just what you need to wrap up your day. You steel yourself and head out. As you clear the door, she meets you and the look on her face isn't making you feel any better.

"Can we talk?" she states curtly.

"Um, sure . . . I have to get to my next . . . thing . . . " you struggle for some illusive schedule conflict.

"Fine, I'll walk with you," she says.

"Okey doke!" you say in a falsely chipper voice as you head for the stairwell and open the door. You make a fundamental air of trying to fill the awkward silence with idle chatter "I thought the meeting went well. I thought Becky had a great idea when she suggested . . . "

As you open the door and step onto the landing Ellen cuts you off, "Who exactly do you think you are that you can decide we are going to include some people's ideas and not others? I mean, really! I'm just about sick of the way you are running this committee!"

You turn to meet her eyes and for the first time realize that she is really mad and unhappy, and it's all directed full force at you! As you struggle to find the words to respond, you look around instinctively for the best way out of this.

First Alternative Path:

If you decide to take a deep breath and try to use your words to work this through, proceed to Path D (see page 83).

Second Alternative Path:

If you decide enough is enough and no one appreciates your effort and you have had it and a good shove down the stairs is just what the Dr. ordered to fix this situation, proceed to Path P (see page 89).

PATH Z

UGH! The easy approach sounds great to you too. You didn't ask for this. You have your own work to do too. So fine! Let's take the path of least resistance and just move through it all as quickly as possible.

"OK! Your right! That sounds great. Let's spend the rest of this meeting discussing those priorities and then we will meet again in two weeks to finalize the goals and then we should have our plan. I will let the director know how the group feels and what we have decided."

As the meeting churns on and the brainstorming narrows down the list of priorities your gut churns. On the one hand you feel a tremendous sense of relief at the notion that you will soon be done with the task and put the plan to bed. On the other, the pit in the bottom of your stomach tells you that letting the director know is probably not going to go all that well. Worse, you feel a sense of loss and disappointment you cannot quite put your finger on. Little did you know that you didn't need to worry as the director was going to be more than happy to pin that feeling down for you.

"Wow! Well, I am surprised and disappointed. I really thought you were the person for the task. I really thought you would take the possibilities of this moment and run with them. I guess I was wrong about you, and the true loss is the library's. Now I have to decide if I let the decision of the committee stand, or if I intervene and force a more creative plan using someone else. Neither will be ideal. If I let it stand, the library staff loses the opportunity to do something really wonderful for our community over the next few years. If I push for a different committee decision, I undermine you and the empowerment I have always tried to give work groups in our organization and end up with a group of people pressured into an effort they feel they don't support. Not the ideal recipe for creativity."

The director sighs heavily as she leans back in her chair. In the ensuing silence you realize you have made a decision that may have taken you from rising star to black hole in the blink of an eye.

The End

If this is not the ending you want for you or your library, go back and take advantage of your "do over" by taking the other Alternative Path—Path E (see page 84).

CHAPTER 13

Conclusion

CHANGE WITHIN YOUR LIBRARY

Unquestionably, this strategic planning process is an energetic endeavor for any library staff to undertake. Encouragingly, the journey is more than worth the investment. The benefits gained by a library organization from investing so much time and human resources in this type of change process are monumental. No process will result in a perfect strategic plan, but the journey will be eye opening at the very least and highly constructive at the very best. Following the planning process will instigate change within the organization. Change is where all progress begins.

This 21st Century Library Strategic Plan Model process will expose strengths and weaknesses within the organization beyond just those related to the mission through the SWOT and STEP analyses. This process is about your people, who they are, what they want, how they work together, and the culture of the organization. All of these things will be revealed by a rigorous strategic planning process. Some organizations don't really want to reveal these characteristics about themselves, but without this understanding an organization cannot move forward to improvement and provide the best possible service to its community (Figure 13.1).

It is very hard to do the work necessary to create a useful plan to help guide your library into the uncertain future, and provide the important services to make your library relevant and valuable in a 21st Century community. It is equally as hard to capitalize on the limited resources available to make that happen, and make every resource, especially human resources, contribute toward that new mission. Organizational change is healthy, and will lead to an organization better positioned to accomplish its new mission.

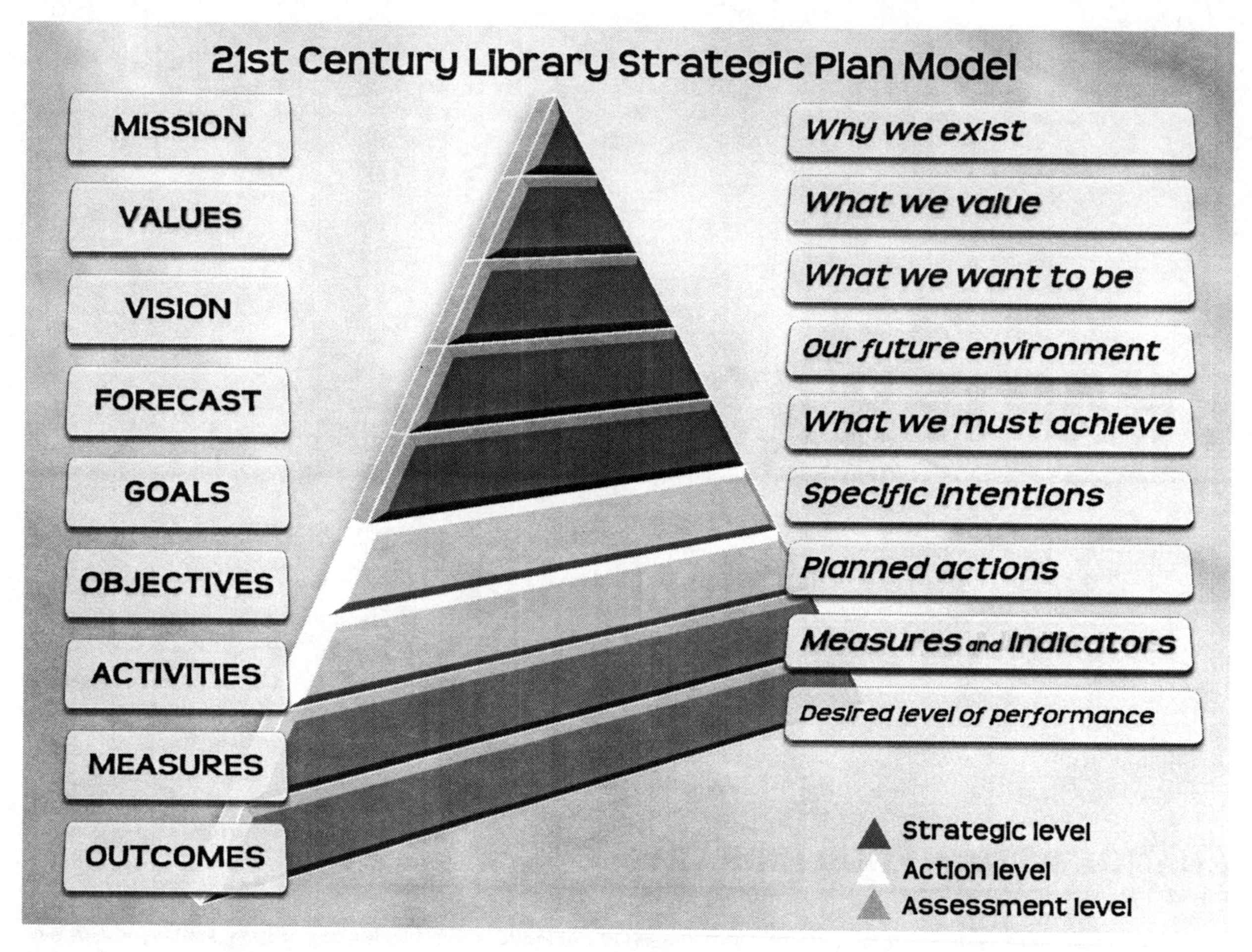

Figure 13.1 Strategic Plan Model

THE PLANNING PROCESS

At various places in this book, reference was made to reviewing and revising elements of the plan after they are developed. Figure 13.2 illustrates the continuous strategic planning process of review and revision of all elements of your strategic plan. For example, when you move on from the development of goals to objectives, the goals are still open to addition, deletion, revision, and review in order for there to be complete compatibility between all the elements of your plan. If you recognize that an important objective more appropriately belongs to a different goal than originally thought, simply revise that goal or add it to your list of goals. The same process is applicable between all elements of the plan.

This process does not stop after you are satisfied with your plan. It happens continuously and whenever you recognize a need for change. The section on incorporating opportunity in Chapter 7, "Goals and Objectives," is a perfect example of when the strategic plan needs to be revised. Any type of opportunity or major change to library operations will most likely impact every element of your plan except the mission. When goals change or are revised, objectives also change as do accompanying activities, associated measures, and outcomes which all impact your resource allocation. Therefore, your strategic plan is by necessity a living document. The members of your staff who are involved with such changes are usually determined by the nature and impact of the changes, but eventually all members of the staff should be informed of the changes to the strategic plan.

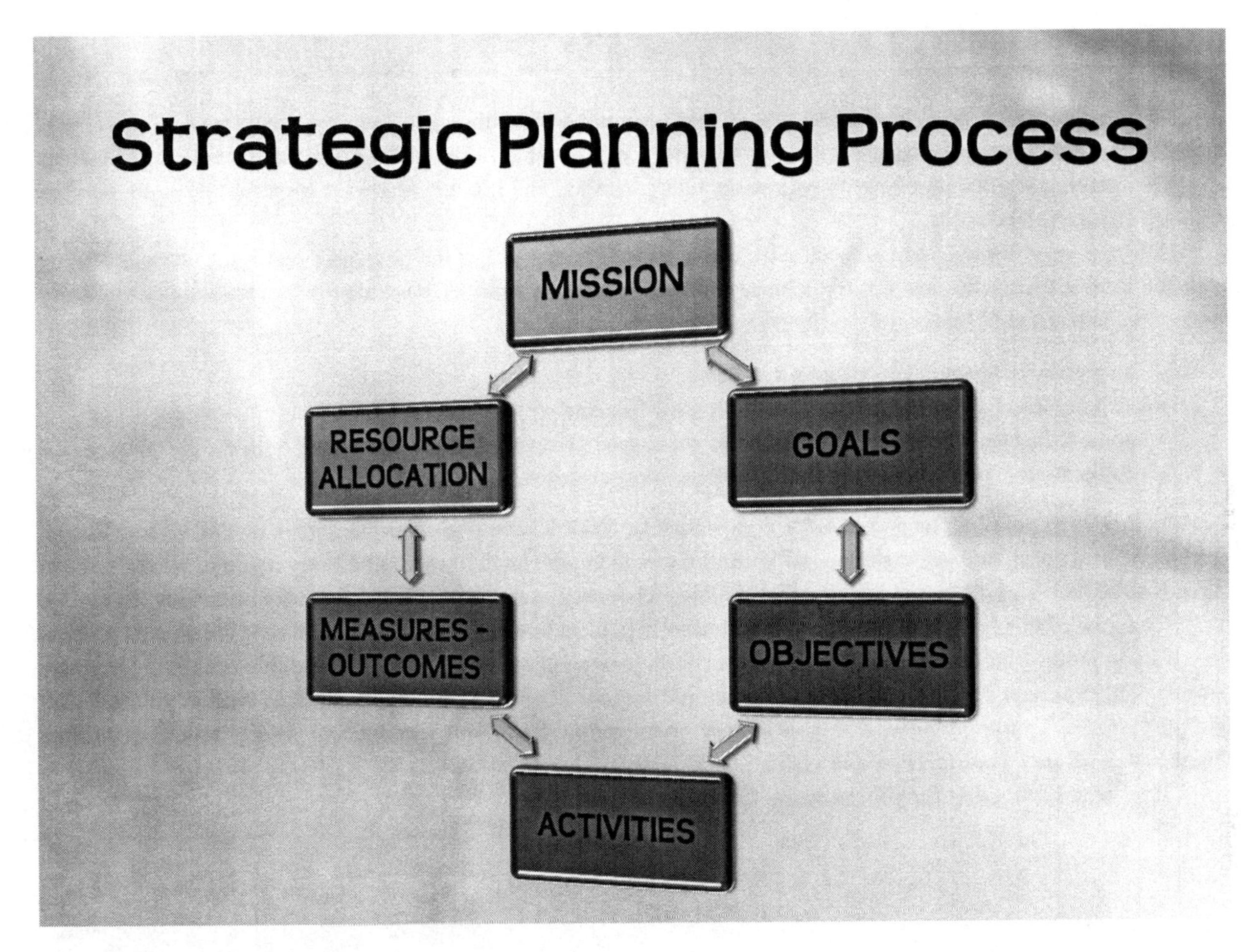

Figure 13.2 Strategic Planning Process

EXECUTION OF YOUR PLAN

One thing you may have questioned about this process was the regimented structure of the process and the resulting plan that may also seem regimented. As noted in Chapter 1, "Why Develop a Strategic Plan," just because the plan seems to create a mechanism so simple that any talking parrot can run a library, it takes much creativity, experience, talent, and even art to actually run the library daily and implement the plan effectively. Which means the plan should not stifle individual initiative, an essential characteristic in any good organization.

The plan will provide guidelines along which supervisors and leaders can direct that individual initiative and creativity, implementing actions to complete activities that achieve objectives that contribute to goals and ultimately the mission's success. Again, without the leader's talent of adapting to the ever-changing external and internal environment, any plan is useless. Equally as important in the implementation is the individual initiative and creativity of staff in solving problems and helping implement the course corrections influenced by environmental changes. Individual initiative and creativity should be core values in every organization that transcend any plan. A thorough understanding of the plan by all members of the organization will ensure that it is kept alive and forefront in daily operations.

All this change will promote improvements in service, and renewed dedication to the organization and its mission, which will unquestionably improve your library's relevance to your community. Being highly relevant and irreplaceable to your community is the best goal any library can achieve. It will ensure your library's survival in the uncertain future of the 21st Century technology advancements and changing social conditions.

BECOMING A 21ST CENTURY LIBRARY

While some think good librarianship is all that is required for a library to forge into the 21st Century future, in reality those things cannot be accomplished by what one learned in library school, even as recently as five years ago. They require significant communication, change, planning, and lifelong learning. Most of all, future success requires visionary leadership.

21st Century librarianship is faced with a new paradigm that places the emphasis on library leaders dealing with the local situation to position their library to thrive, not just survive. That requires exceptionally visionary leadership. What would it take for the library:

- to regain its former stature and importance;
- to be recognized as the primary institution for free and equitable access for all to information;
- to be the place where people turn first to get answers to everyday questions; and
- to be the location where they find life altering experiences?

Is that even possible, or desirable? Unquestionably, YES! The real problem becomes one of vision. Vision, entrepreneurial spirit, and leadership are all essential to making the local library **the** library again in whatever form it needs to be in this 21st Century society. Developing a visionary strategic plan is the first step in making it a reality.

The goal of this book is to provide you with a solid plan and essential strategy to embrace the change process necessary to guide your library and its staff into becoming an organization prepared and capable of thriving in a new century. The plan you develop will serve to communicate your library's vision and values, as well as your mission and all the other building blocks of a great library organization. How well you execute your plan will determine whether you achieve your mission and vision.

Everyone is cheering for your success. Good Luck!

BIBLIOGRAPHY

Brown, M. "Improving Your Organization's Vision." *Journal for Quality & Participation* 21, no. 5 (1998): 18.

Chermack, T., and B. Kasshanna. "The Use and Misuse of SWOT Analysis and Implications for HRD Professionals." *Human Resource Development International* 10, no. 4 (2007): 383–99.

Drake, B. *Poll Finds a "Perfect Storm" of Voter Distrust in Government*. New York: Huffington Post Politics, 2010. http://www.politicsdaily.com/2010/04/18/poll-finds-a-perfect-storm-of-voter-distrust-in-government/.

Feinman, V. "Five Steps Toward Planning Today for Tomorrow's Needs." *Computers in Libraries* 19, no. 1 (1999): 18.

Frost, R. *Mountain Interval*. New York: Henry Holt and Company, 1920.

Gross, D. "The Perfect Storm That Could Drown the Economy." *NYTimes.com*, May 8, 2005. http://www.nytimes.com/2005/05/08/weekinreview/08gross.html?_r=2.

Hall, S., D. Lovallo, and R. Musters. "How to Put Your Money Where Your Strategy Is." *McKinsey Quarterly*, no. 2 (2012): 27–38.

Institute of Museum and Library Services (IMLS). "Outcome-Based Evaluation (OBE)." http://www.imls.gov/applicants/basics.aspx.

Johnson, J., and A. Smith. *60 Minute Strategic Plan*. Gold River, CA: 60 Minute Strategic Plan, Inc., 2006.

Junger, S. *The Perfect Storm: A True Story of Men Against the Sea*. New York: W.W. Norton & Company, Inc., 1997.

Kidd, J. R. *How Adults Learn*. New York: Association Press, 1973.

Kotter, J.P. "Leading Change: Why Transformation Efforts Fail." *Harvard Business Review* 73, no. 2 (1995): 59–67.

Lucas, J. "Anatomy of a Vision Statement." *Management Review* 87, no. 2 (1998): 22.

Meyer, P. "What Would You Do If You Knew You Couldn't Fail? Creating S.M.A.R.T. Goals," in *Attitude Is Everything: If You Want to Succeed Above and Beyond*, 12–22. Waco, TX: Meyer Resource Group, Incorporated, 2003.

Miller, D. "Successful Change Leaders: What Makes Them? What Do They Do That Is Different?" *Journal of Change Management* 2, no. 4 (2002): 359–68.

National Library Service for the Blind and Physically Handicapped, The Library of Congress, 2012, http://www.loc.gov/nls/.

Nelson, S. *Strategic Planning for Results*. Chicago: ALA Press, 2008.

Parman, A. "The Big Picture: Strategic Planning and Interpretive Master Planning." *OMA Dispatch*, http://aparman.com/articles/bigpicture/.

Pells, D. "Commitment to Ethics and Values Can Empower Leaders of Teams, Projects, Programs and Organizations." *PM World Today* 14, no. 1 (2012): 1–7.

Safian, R. *This Is Generation Flux: Meet the Pioneers of the New (and Chaotic) Frontier of Business*. New York: Fast Company Magazine, Mansueto Ventures LLC, 2012. http://www.fastcompany.com/1802732/generation-flux-meet-pioneers-new-and-chaotic-frontier-business.

Samples, M. *The Perfect Storm: Today's Economy Creates Favorable Conditions for Sale-leaseback Sellers*. Chicago: Commercial Investment Real Estate Magazine, 2005. http://www.ccim.com/cire-magazine/articles/perfect-storm.

Sukovic, S. "Strategically Creative: A Case of the Library Planning Process." *Journal of Organisational Transformation and Social Change* 8, no. 3 (2011): 261–79.

Topeka & Shawnee County (KS) Public Library, 2012 Mission Statement, http://tscpl.org/about/strategic-plan/.

Verma, H. "Mission Statements: A Study of Intent and Influence." *Journal of Services Research* 9, no. 2 (2009): 153–72.

Wikipedia, "PEST Analysis." The Wikimedia Foundation, Inc., 2012. http://en.wikipedia.org/wiki/PEST_analysis.

INDEX

Activities, xi, 2, 8, 15, 18, 44–49, 51–56, 57–62, 64, 67–73, 77

Brown, M., 28
Build consensus, 10, 17
Buy-in, 5, 10, 12, 49–50

Chang, M., 2
Change, xiii–xiv, 1–5, 7, 9, 11, 14, 18, 35, 50, 54, 59–60, 64, 93–96
  agent, xiv, 4
  derailment, 18–19
  organizational, xiii–xiv, 2, 31, 93
Choose Your Strategic Plan Ending, 79
Communication, 10–11, 25, 43, 50, 96
Cornell University Library, 50

Derailment, 2, 4, 11, 18, 25, 31, 39, 49, 55, 64, 71, 78
Drake, B., 34

Feinman, V., 2
Forecast, xiii, 1, 3, 7–9, 33–40, 75, 78, 95
  external factors, xiii, 1, 3, 7–8, 33–35, 37–39, 95
  internal factors, 1, 7–8, 33–34, 95
  perfect storm, 33–34

Goals, xi–xiv, 1–4, 8, 10, 15, 18, 31, 33, 38, 41–50, 52, 55, 57–58, 64, 67, 73, 75, 94
  and Objectives, examples, 50
  Cornell University Library, 50
  incorporating opportunity, 47, 94
  Oak Park (IL) Public Library, 50
  planned abandonment, 47
  sample, 48–49
  Seattle (WA) Public Library, 50
  Southwestern Oregon Community College, 50
Gross, D., 34

Hall, Lovallo, and Musters, 68

Institute of Museum and Library Services, 57

Johnson and Smith, xii

Kidd, J., xii
Kotter, J., xiv

Leader, Leadership, xii, xiv, 2–5, 9–12, 17, 19, 23, 25, 32, 36–37, 39–40, 46–47, 50, 53, 55, 70, 78, 80, 95–96
Library
  academic, xiv, 16, 28, 55
  board, xiii, 3, 15, 17, 19, 38–39, 61, 69, 71–72, 74–75, 78
  culture, 25, 28
  external environment, xiii, 1, 3, 7, 35, 89
  internal environment, 2, 37, 89
  public, 3, 15–16, 28, 30, 41, 50, 75
  resources, xi, 2, 9, 40, 51, 68
  school, 16, 19, 28, 75, 96
  staff, xiii, 2–3, 5, 10, 22–23, 39–40, 42, 46, 50, 51–56, 63, 65, 69–72, 73–75, 94
  team, xi, 10–12, 17, 72, 74
  21st Century, xi–xii, 13, 15, 18, 28, 41, 49, 54, 76
Lucas, J., 27

Measures, xii, 8–9, 31, 49, 57–65, 67, 71, 76–77, 94
  examples, 62
  outcomes, the difference, 58
Meyer, P., 44
Miller, D., xiv
Mission, xi–xii, 1–2, 5, 7–8, 10, 21, 27, 31, 33, 41–42, 47–51, 55, 58, 67, 69–71, 73, 93–96
  irrelevant, 11
  organizational influences, 17
  prescribed, 17–18
  relevant, 1, 5, 11, 39
  statement, 13–19
  statement template, 13–14
  21st Century, 14, 18

National Library Service, 18
Nelson, S., 19

Oak Park (IL) Public Library, 50
Objectives, xi–xiv, 2–4, 8, 10, 15–16, 18–19, 33, 38, 41–50, 52, 54–56, 58, 61–62, 67–69, 75–76, 78, 94
  incorporating opportunity, 47, 94
  SMART approach, 44, 49–50
Organizational
  change, xiii–xiv, 2, 31, 93
  culture, 21
  influences, 17
  meeting, 12
  strengths, 52, 107
  values, 25
  weaknesses, 40, 78
Outcomes, xii, 8–9, 33, 44, 49, 54, 57–65, 67, 76–77, 94
  indicators, 57, 61
  outcome-based evaluation (OBE), 57
  target, 61, 64

Parman, A., xii
Patton, G., 2
Pells, D., 23
Perfect storm, 33–34
Prioritize
  activities, 47
  goals and objectives, 1, 4, 53
  resources, 69, 72

Resource allocation, 9, 47, 49, 54, 62, 67–73, 77, 94
  calculations, 68
  costs, 68
  example, 68
  personnel, 69

Safian, R., 34
Samples, M., 34
Seattle (WA) Public Library, 50
Shortcuts, 3, 7, 9, 11, 16, 55
Small Library Ideas, 4, 11, 19, 26, 31, 40, 50, 56, 65, 72, 78
SouthwesternOregon Community College, 50
Stakeholders, xi, 1, 3, 5, 11, 18–19, 40
STEP analysis, 3, 7, 35–36, 39–40, 93
  economic factors, 36
  incorporating results, 38
  political factors, 36
  societal factors, 35
  technological factors, 35
Strategic plan
  activities, xi, 2, 8, 15, 18, 44–49, 51–56, 57–62, 64, 67–72, 73, 77
  appendices, 75, 78
  change, 2
  Choose Your Ending, 79
  document, 38
  example, 75
  execution, 95
  goals, 41–42
  importance, 2
  measures, 58
  mission, xi–xii, 1–2, 5, 7–8, 10, 13–19, 41–42, 47–50, 69–71, 93–96
  objectives, 41–42
  organization, 73–78
  outcomes, 58
  public version, 76, 78
  roadmap, 3, 10, 34
  successful, xi–xii
  values, 21–26
  vision, 27
  why, 1–3, 8
Strategic planning process, xii–xiii, 3–5, 7, 10–11, 16–17, 22–23, 30–31, 35, 38–40, 43–44, 47, 49–50, 53, 55–56, 61, 70, 72, 79, 93–96
Sukovic, S., xii
SWOT analysis, 5, 37–40, 93
  incorporating results, 38
  opportunities, 38
  strengths, 37
  threats, 38
  weaknesses, 37

Topeka & Shawnee County (KS) Public Library, 18
21st Century
  becoming a 21st Century library, 96
  community, 4–5, 41, 50, 93
  environment, xi-xii, 27, 33, 38–39, 41, 48
  future, 8, 27, 50, 96
  goals and objectives, 15
  influences, 25
  librarianship, 15, 96
  library, xi–xii, 13, 15, 18, 28, 41, 49, 54, 76
  mission, 18

technology, 18, 95
vision, xiv, 28
21st Century Library Strategic Plan Model, 8–9, 13, 32, 41, 44, 58, 67, 93
benefits, 10
components, 8
derailment, 11
why, 7

Values, 8–10, 14, 28, 31–33, 42, 61, 70, 75, 78, 95–96
and Guiding Principles, 21–26, 32
descriptors, 24
examples, 24
organizational, 25
statement, 13, 21, 24–25
Verma, H., 15
Vision, 27
descriptors, 29–30
library, 27–28
The Question, 31
sample statement, 31
statement, xii, 8, 10, 21, 33

Where are we now, 16
Why we exist, xii, 8, 13–14, 16, 18–19, 21, 27, 33
Wikipedia, 35

ABOUT THE AUTHORS

STEPHEN A. MATTHEWS has been a Rural Library Consultant at the Utah State Library for the past six years where he consults with numerous small and rural library staff and boards. He was instrumental in guiding the State Library during its recent development of a new Strategic Plan. Steve earned his PhD in Adult, Occupational and Continuing Education from Kansas State University, and in 1996 his Master of Library Science at Emporia State University. His first master's degree is in Systems Management from University of Southern California. As a U.S. Army officer, Steve's first career was followed by positions as a training director for a NASA program, a college dean, and a director of research. In Kansas, he and his wife owned Matthews Education Consulting where they provided consulting and training in education technology, and developed technology-based educational products for the local school district. 21st Century Librarianship is now his interest.

KIMBERLY D. MATTHEWS has led the Trenton (NJ) Free Public Library as the executive director for the past five years through two downsizings due to budget cuts of nearly 50%. She has reengineered all internal processes for increased fiscal responsibility and economy of resources, and implemented new policies for all areas of service and operation. She has served as a Board Member of LYRASIS, and Central NJ Regional Library Cooperative. Kimberly earned her MLS from Emporia State University in 1994, and later earned an MBA from University of Phoenix. Her library career has included positions in all types of libraries, and unique experience with the Smithsonian, NASA, Washington State University, and several public library systems. Before Trenton, Kimberly spent nearly a decade on the management team for the award winning Salt Lake City Public Library. Among her numerous responsibilities she chaired the Planning Committee that crafted SLCPL's ground-breaking 2007–2009 Strategic Plan.